GOD, T[HE BIBLE]
AND THE
INDIVIDUAL

Ulf Ekman

Word of Life Publications

GOD, THE STATE AND THE INDIVIDUAL
First published in English, 1990
Second printing, 1993

ISBN 91 7866 133 1
ISBN 1 884017 08 8 USA

Original Swedish edition, copyright © 1988
Ulf Ekman. All rights reserved

English translation, copyright © 1990 Ulf Ekman

Printed in Finland for Word of Life Publications
by TryckPartner AB

Word of Life Publications
Box 17, S-751 03 Uppsala, Sweden
Box 46108, Minneapolis, MN 55446, USA
Box 641, Marine Parade, Singapore 9144

Acknowledgments
Unless otherwise indicated, Scripture quotations are
from the *Holy Bible, New International Version,*
copyright © 1973, 1978, 1984 International Bible Society.
Used by permission of Zondervan Bible Publishers

Other scripture quotations are from the *New King James
Version* of the Bible (NKJV), copyright © 1979, 1980, 1982
Thomas Nelson Publishers, Inc.; *The Living Bible* (TLB),
copyright © 1971 Tyndale House Publishers

Dedicated to the new generation of uncompromising believers who will take the Gospel to the ends of the earth and carry the power of God to every nation.

Special thanks to Tore and Birgit who were kind enough to have me as a guest and allow me to write this book in the peace and quiet of their home.

Daniel answered and said, "Blessed be the name of God forever and ever, for wisdom and might are His. And He changes the times and the seasons; He removes kings and raises up kings; He gives wisdom to the wise and knowledge to those who have understanding. He reveals deep and secret things; He knows what is in the darkness and light dwells with Him."

Daniel 2:20-22, NKJV

Contents

Preface

Sweden is a wonderful country. However, it is also a country in crisis. Its crisis is spiritual, social, political and economic.

We must realize, though, that like every nation, Sweden has a calling from God. It is a call to return to Him and become His instrument in spreading His glory throughout the earth. The Gospel is full of God's glory and power, and it is God's will that entire nations should bear this glory.

Sweden, however, has been weighed in the balance and found wanting. But glory to God, His mercy is greater than the sum of Sweden's sins and iniquities. I am convinced that God is able to change the spiritual atmosphere of this country and make Sweden what He desires it to be—a beacon of power and life for the world.

We do not need to wonder at the spiritual warfare that is taking place over this land. Is it because Sweden is somehow more special than other countries? No, but it is vital that we take our place in God's global plan and do our part in speeding the return of Jesus Christ—that we preach the Gospel of Jesus followed by signs and wonders, across the face of the earth.

This book reveals the way God deals, not only with individuals, but with nations, their rulers and governments; and the Church in relation to these.

God is raising up His Church today as a powerful tool to address individuals, nations and the spirit world. The prophetic word of God will again shake society and turn the world upside down. This will create the necessary conditions for the glorious revival that will sweep through the face of the earth prior to the return of Jesus Christ.

Ulf Ekman

1

The Foundations of Freedom

Before we can begin to discuss the responsibility of the Church and the individual believer in relation to rulers and authorities, we must define a concept of great importance—the idea of freedom. Freedom is a word that is used by many people with a variety of different meanings. However, we must understand its true meaning—what it is and what it is not.

Freedom has been celebrated, exalted and discussed throughout the ages. It is fundamental to human life and lies deeply embedded within our nature. The loss of freedom is virtually unbearable, and throughout the course of history men and women have given their lives to preserve this precious phenomenon.

To some, freedom is the ability to be left alone, while for others it is being able to be with other people. To many, it simply means having freedom of choice. To others, it means not being controlled or told what to do. Different political parties give the word different connotations, but wherever freedom is mentioned, the response is positive.

Freedom is something precious and valuable. Strangely enough, though, it is a word that has scarcely been heard in our political debates during the past few years. It is hardly a word that appears regularly on the front page of the paper, or has a place in our everyday vocabulary.

Words like "security," "equality" and "community" appear more frequently, but these words or phenomena would be unknown to us were it not for the foundational concept of "freedom," that exists as their prerequisite and basis.

The Dangers of Conformity

What, then, is freedom? It has been implanted in every human being by God Himself. He created each individual as a unique person and he made us to live in freedom. Everyone has been created free and with qualities no one else possesses.

God has a special plan for every person, a specific task that only that person can accomplish. Each of us has an entirely unique personal worth. God is creative. He does not mass-produce us on an assembly line, but makes every one of us differently. He can afford variety, since freedom is a part of His nature, and freedom always expresses itself in variation.

The type of conformity that causes people to think alike, dress alike, drive the same kind of car and never dare to diverge from the opinion of the majority does not come from God.

There is a certain security in conformity and uniformity with the crowd, and the fear of standing out causes many people to hold back and keep quiet. Such repressed behavior is not from God. It has been externally imposed on people to the point that they dare not take personal initiatives without receiving orders from a person in a position of superiority.

Monopolized television and welfare boards recommend what we should think, what we should eat and what we ought to do in our leisure time. When our authorities issue the decree that the entire country is to be taxed, we bow in subservience. Though we may secretly clench our fists, we accept the decree simply because it comes from above.

While such commandments are accepted without question, divergent opinions from a "non-authoritative" source feel threatening. They disturb our so-called "unity" and "security" and, because they are non-conformist, we think that they cannot really be trusted. Deep down, however, people are not at all this way. It is merely imposed behavior from which they can, and will, be free.

Christian Faith Brings True Freedom

In Luke 4:16-19, we see something tremendous happen as Jesus preaches in the synagogue in Nazareth and opens the scroll to read from Isaiah 61. He proclaims that the Spirit of the Lord is over Him and He specifies the task to which He has been called:

> The Spirit of the Lord is on me because he has anointed me to preach good news to the poor. He has sent me to proclaim freedom for the prisoners and recovery of sight for the blind, to release the oppressed, to proclaim the year of the Lord's favor (Luke 4:18-19).

The word "freedom" is mentioned twice in verse 18: "freedom for the prisoners" and "to release (set free) the oppressed." Freedom is obviously something meaningful to God. It is so valuable that Jesus emphasizes it as He clarifies His purpose here on earth. All that Jesus said and did while He was here was done with the express purpose of giving people freedom.

In John 8:36 Jesus says, If the Son sets you free, you will be free indeed. The freedom that Jesus talks about here is true freedom. The Gospel is the good news that Jesus Christ of Nazareth died on the cross and paid the price for the sin and guilt of mankind.

The Bible says that God created man to live in freedom and to fellowship with Him, but man fell into sin instead. Man's sin was a conscious choice to rebel against God. As a result, he was lost and his fellowship with God was destroyed. Although he was once free, he became a slave to sin and was taken captive by the devil. His spiritual life was ruined and he began to experience captivity in every area of his being.

Jesus states, *I tell you the truth, everyone who sins is a slave to sin* (John 8:34). Jesus died on Calvary to deliver us from this captivity and its terrifying consequences in every area of our lives:

> So that by his death he might destroy him who holds the power of death—that is, the devil—and free those who all their lives were held in slavery by their fear of death (Heb 2:14-15).

The Gospel is a Declaration of Independence

Jesus came to bring freedom to the captives! The entire Gospel is an emancipation proclamation. Galatians 3:13-14 says that we have been "redeemed." Through the death of Jesus, there is complete freedom from sin and its many consequences. Because of His death, we can know redemption, liberation and freedom from the collar of slavery. Once again, we are free men!

When Jesus preached in the synagogue in Nazareth, He declared this freedom by proclaiming a year of mercy from the Lord. He was referring to the year of jubilee mentioned in Leviticus 25:10:

> Consecrate the fiftieth year and *proclaim liberty throughout the land* to all its inhabitants. It shall be a jubilee for you; each one of you is to return to his family property and each to his own clan.

This is exactly what Jesus proclaimed—freedom and restoration! The devil has stolen what belongs to man and has made him a slave. Slavery, irrespective of which area of life it affects, comes from the devil and not from God.

The freedom that Jesus offers us cost Him an incredible amount. No one will be able to fully understand or appreciate the price that He paid on Calvary. It was immense! However, the freedom of humanity is worth such a great deal to God, that He was willing to pay the necessary price. Freedom is extremely precious, therefore we must do our utmost to preserve it:

> It is for freedom that Christ has *set us free*. Stand firm, then, and do not let yourselves be burdened again by a yoke of slavery (Gal 5:1).

Freedom is precious. Partly because God made it an inherent part of creation and intended every individual to live in it, and partly because Jesus had to pay a huge price to redeem mankind and restore his fellowship with God. Freedom is an integral part of every human being, and until it is experienced, neither an individual nor a nation will know true happiness. Just as a fish is made for water, we are created for freedom; we will not be satisfied with anything else, no matter what we are told.

Freedom Without Chaos

A non-Christian, someone whose foundation is not in God, usually imagines freedom to simply mean "freedom of choice" or "independence." There is an element of truth in both expressions; but when the Bible uses the word "freedom", it entails much more than this.

To God, freedom is more than mere independence. There is a counterfeit independence that destroys human life. People rebel against God with the false assumption that this will produce independence, but they only become slaves instead. Many people say, "I can do whatever I want—no one is going to tell me what to do." This may sound good, but it is purely egocentric and nothing more than rebellion toward God.

When we refer to freedom, we do not mean a freedom of choice that lets us choose whatever we want, as long as we make a choice. This type of "freedom" is completely without foundation and leads only to chaos. If 75% of the population were to decide that burglary and murder are acceptable forms of behavior, they may be demonstrating their freedom to express an opinion, but they would hardly make burglary or murder right.

Freedom is not subjective or relative. It is objective and eternal and founded in God—in who He is and what He has said. His commandments are called, *the perfect law that gives freedom* (Jas 1:25). In other words, the law of God not only protects and preserves freedom, it also sets people free.

In John 8:31-32 Jesus says,

> If you hold to my teaching (the Word of God), you are really my disciples. Then you will know the truth, and the *truth will set you free.*

Freedom is not genuine if truth is absent. The function of truth is to set people free. The freedom God's Word describes is the truth of who God is, what He has and what He can do, as well as who you are, what you have and what you can do in Christ. It is also the truth regarding who your enemy is, what he has and what he can do.

Freedom is not merely independence. No one is an isolated island who can live solely for himself. Freedom comes when you enter your true function in life. Just as a car cannot maintain its freedom when water is poured in the gas tank—in spite of how free you may be to do so—people cannot be free until they find their place in God.

Freedom is being and doing what you were created for. Therefore, there is no true freedom for nations or individuals outside of God. True freedom comes only through submission and obedience to God. Rebellion toward Him brings nothing but bondage, in spite of how free you may think you are.

Freedom for Nations

An individual who receives Jesus as his Lord and Savior receives a tremendous amount of freedom. As the Spirit of God takes up residence in him, his spirit, or inner man, is born again. The experience of salvation and new birth is the greatest thing that can ever happen to someone.

> Where the Spirit of the Lord is, there is *freedom* (2 Cor 3:17).

Freedom begins in your life as soon as the Spirit of God comes into you. God wants the spiritual life, which you receive through the Holy Spirit, to permeate your entire being, your life and your surroundings. He wants you to walk in the Spirit, manifesting freedom in every area of your life. Abundant life from God can then pulsate through you, to create freedom all around you.

Freedom is not just internal, it affects every area of life. Likewise, where God's life is missing, there is bondage, both individually and collectively, as well as spiritually, socially, financially and politically. Freedom is available for captives in every area of life, and where the Gospel has success, every area of human existence is affected.

This has all too often been misunderstood. Certain groups have begun to present a politicized, "social" version of the Gospel in response to teaching which has denied the power in the Word of God. As a result, the Gospel is presented as something purely internal and without external results. Salvation no longer involves the spiritual regeneration of an individual, but rather a revolutionary change of power, for example.

Although it may contain Christian words, this type of Gospel is false and often preached by people who are themselves spiritually unregenerate. Jesus did not come with political slogans, He came to save lost souls. The Spirit of God will also change and uplift nations, through believers. This cannot happen through a liberal or "social" Gospel, in which huge portions of the Bible are deleted and the supernatural is rejected.

Much of contemporary Christianity has been deliberately corrupted and soured by such tendencies, especially during the last twenty years. The effects of this have been devastating.

A great deal of "denial theology" has been spread from liberal educational institutions to the Church, which has become weakened as a result. The Bible has been criticized, torn apart and denied to the point that many Christians are ashamed to take Jesus literally or to do what He has said. At times, there have been colossal attacks against the supernatural element of Christianity.

Everything Jesus and the early apostles did in the power of the Holy Spirit has been mocked, even though it was considered normal for them and should, therefore, be normal for us today. But times are changing. In spite of what our theological institutions say, the Spirit of God is creating a new freedom. Thousands are emerging from spiritual captivity, refusing to accept the wishy-washy, poisoned food they have been served.

Proclaim the Gospel of Freedom!

Believers will no longer tolerate the Church of God being infiltrated by the system of the world—with its flood of worldly explanations and authoritarian demands for blind subjection to a leadership that is politically secularized and backslidden.

A new generation is rising to take possession of the land. It will proclaim the Gospel of liberty and the power of God to bring change and freedom in every area of life. Much of the spiritual freedom that has been in danger of total extinction in the last twenty years is returning. The spiritual climate is definitely changing.

In spite of loud protests from a disappearing minority, the full Gospel of Jesus Christ is being proclaimed more strongly than ever before and God is confirming His Word with signs and wonders, just as He has promised.

2

The Concept of Authority

Mankind has been created for freedom, though not for freedom at the expense of others. Freedom was not made available for man to live an egocentric, selfish life of sensual pleasure, but so that he could find his true position and begin to operate in it.

God created man and expected his submission so that freedom could become a reality in his life. God has established certain laws and order which exist to bring about and preserve all that He desires. Where there is no order there is only chaos. Order can be compared to a mold in which something is to be cast. Without the mold, the substance pours out and there is no lasting result.

God is concerned primarily with three orders, or institutions:

The first is marriage. The successful working of society is based on the success of marriage, which is the oldest institution. Chaos in relationships and within the family structure affect an entire country. One of the most effective ways that the devil attacks a nation is through undermining and dissolving marriages and the nucleus of the family.

The second institution is the Church. This has a crucial position in the world. If the Church fails to function properly, nothing else will. The Church is the mediator of the glory, the presence, the power and the revelation of God to the entire world. If the Church is disordered or backslidden and loses its saltiness, it is not good for anything.

The Church has no other function than to bring the Gospel and the power of God to the world so the world can be saved. If it fails to do this, it has missed its objective, regardless of whatever else it may be doing.

So called "cultural" Christianity, which lacks the teaching of repentance, is an extremely effective tool through which the enemy can create a whole generation of Pharisees. These people are active within the Church but lack their own personal salvation. The resulting outer varnish of culture and religion has vaccinated the masses against the true Gospel and becomes a curse for humanity. Because of this, people are held captive rather than being set free.

The third institution is government, or a variety of different governing authorities. In this chapter we will center our attention on this institution.

Authority is Designated by God

People have always needed some form of government, and it has always existed, in one form or another. In Romans 13, Paul discusses governing authorities. These scriptures have often been pushed aside, but they are significant and need to be understood.

> Everyone must submit himself to the governing authorities, for there is no authority except that which God has established. The authorities that exist have been established by God. Consequently, he who rebels against the authority is rebelling against what God has instituted, and those who do so will bring judgment

on themselves. For rulers hold no terror for those who do right, but for those who do wrong. Do you want to be free from fear of the one in authority? Then do what is right and he will commend you. For he is God's servant to do you good. But if you do wrong, be afraid, for he does not bear the sword for nothing. He is God's servant, an agent of wrath to bring punishment on the wrongdoer. Therefore, it is necessary to submit to the authorities, not only because of possible punishment but also because of conscience. This is also why you pay taxes, for the authorities are God's servants, who give their full time to governing. Give everyone what you owe him: If you owe taxes, pay taxes; if revenue, then revenue; if respect, then respect; if honor then honor (Rom 13:1-7).

What is Paul saying here? He is telling us that our government is an earthly institution that has been ordained by God. As with the family and the Church, God has laid down certain limitations and regulations, so that society will not collapse in a state of chaos. Authorities are a part of this order.

As an institution, governing authorities have been ordained by God. This does not imply, however, that everyone in a position of authority has been ordained by God and can, therefore, do as he wishes. The Scripture states that the institution of government itself has been ordained by God for a specific purpose.

When it fulfills this purpose, it carries out a service (Rom 13:6), just like the father who brings up his children or the pastor who preaches the Word to the Church.

People in authority, parents and pastors alike, can abuse their positions or neglect to carry out the tasks they have been given. Each of these three institutions must understand their purpose, or the type of commission they have received, so they do neither more nor less than what they have been ordained to do.

We must understand that these institutions are God-given. They exist to prevent chaos and as a channel of God's blessings to all men. Against this background, we can begin to understand the destructive tendencies that cause people to rebel against and break up these institutions, causing the loss of both life and power.

The Purpose of Government

As a foundational institution the government exists to carry out certain tasks, and in Romans 13 Paul clearly states what these are. The government is to:

1. Uphold the law (v. 3).
2. Protect law-abiding citizens (v. 3).
3. Punish wrongdoers (vv. 2,4).
4. Uphold external and internal defense (v. 4). (The sword was a defensive weapon against external and internal threats and, at that time, soldiers carried out both of these tasks. Today we have police to preserve internal law and order, and national defense to secure external order.)
5. Collect taxes (v. 6).

Those who are in authority have received a mandate to carry out these tasks. Therefore, we should not resist them (v. 2), but accept them as necessary for our nation's well-being and continued existence (vv. 5-7).

If the government was prevented from exercising its power; from legislating and putting laws into effect and carrying out its commission, the entire community would enter a state of chaos and anarchy.

Individuals would do whatever suited them at the moment, with no means of restraint. Since mankind is fundamentally self-centered, the result would be utter confusion.

The Biblical view of man as a social creature within society, shows us that without God he is selfish, sinful, rebellious and on the road to eternal destruction as a result of his fall into sin. Law and order are necessary because we live in a fallen world.

If thieves did not exist, we would have no need for locks or policemen. Today, however, no one would be foolish enough to dispute their necessity, whether they have faith in God or not. The law would not be needed if it were not broken. But because it is broken, it must exist and be implemented.

Our Relationship with the Law

We know that the law is good if one uses it properly. We also know that law is made not for the righteous but for lawbreakers and rebels, the ungodly and sinful, the unholy and irreligious; for those who kill their fathers or mothers, for murderers, for adulterers and perverts, for slave traders and liars and perjurers— and for whatever else is contrary to the sound doctrine (1 Tim 1:8-10).

This does not imply that believers are free from the law in the sense that they can do whatever they want. It means that, as believers, we have the Spirit of God within us, who causes us to follow prescribed laws and ordinances.

Burglary is not a Christian practice. The Spirit of God supernaturally changes people so they no longer desire to steal, making the law which forbids theft inapplicable. The law is automatically adhered to by the indwelling Spirit of God.

On New Year's Eve 1988, a group of 1,000 young people rioted on the streets of Helsingborg, Sweden, breaking shop windows, stealing goods and causing extensive damage.

At exactly the same time, approximately 3,000 young people gathered in the city of Uppsala to praise God and pray in the New Year. Not a chair was broken and nothing was stolen. Why? Because the Spirit of God was within them!

The first event was reported in the papers. The second was overlooked in silence, in spite of the fact that Uppsala had never before seen such a New Year's Eve gathering.

As long as there are those who are not yet reconciled to God through faith in the Gospel of Jesus Christ, there will be problems and authorities will be needed to uphold law and order. Without them, chaos is the inevitable result and a situation that eventually leads to the direct opposite, a form of tyranny or dictatorship.

Legislation Based on Truth

A government should not, and indeed cannot, rule at its own discretion. It has received a commission that has limitations. Problems arise when authorities do not recognize that their commission is from God, or when they fail to realize its limitations.

Authorities legislate and implement laws. The legislative process in itself is good, but on what foundation should this process be built?

In a society where God's existence and standard of morality is acknowledged, there exists an acceptable ground for legislation. If a society recognizes that God has given mankind certain human rights, which are to be protected and promoted through the placement of authorities, then those in authority have found their rightful position.

However, when the existence of God is denied, together with the rights He has given mankind as expressed in the Ten Commandments, a government ends up following an arbitrary relativism. This eventually leads to manipulation and the abuse of power.

When authorities begin to legislate laws that are contrary to God's laws, they legislate lawlessness and place that country in a dangerous and vulnerable position. Therefore, the foundation of all legislation is extremely important. If it is relative and arbitrary, society will eventually collapse in a state of chaos, which will damage the entire nation.

Many countries in the western world operate under a democracy. We should be thankful for it and preserve this form of government. However, the majority of countries in the world do not have a democracy, but rather some form of dictatorship, either communist or fascist.

A democratic society should not be taken for granted. Those of us who enjoy such freedom should thank God for it, because it is extremely precious!

The principles of democracy have their historical roots in the Judeo-Christian tradition. The expansion and influence of Christianity in European societies have created the conditions necessary for our modern democracies. The Bible and faith in the Word of God, as an objective and valid truth, has played a large part in our legislation. Furthermore, it has created an environment that has influenced the development of the modern constitutional state.

Even if the average citizen was not personally converted or born again, there was once a strong consciousness of God's existence and a respect for His commandments and laws, (although this respect was occasionally full of hypocrisy and double morality).

Times Have Changed

Today, however, the situation is completely different. We live in a strongly pluralistic society with a highly relative view of our existence. People are brought up merely to become life-oriented rather than to have any sort of personal conviction. Those who do take a stand do so according to personal taste and liking, avoiding any form of general directive or standard.

"If indeed everything is relative," current worldly thinking goes, "why should one view be more correct than another?"

If a person wants to be a punk-rocker or a scientologist, a spiritist or a new-ager, an atheist or a believer, that decision is based on their emotional make-up, their experiences and their personal tastes. It is nor based on an objective truth that defines what is right and what is wrong.

This is the society in which we all live, and to some extent we must accept it. The government has to safeguard the rights of every citizen, regardless of that persons world view or faith. Anything less inevitably becomes some form of dictatorship— whether it be atheistic or religious.

The role of the state is not to legislate salvation for its citizens (as in a religious unitarian society), nor is it to legislate against the possibility of salvation for its citizens. (We will return to the Church and its relationship with the state in the following chapter.)

On the other hand, we must see that the state is incapable of fulfilling its God-given task without God as the foundation in all it does. The human rights, which the state is to protect and promote, have been embedded in humanity by God Himself.

These freedoms and rights include: freedom of opinion, freedom of the press, freedom of trade, right to personal security and safety, right of ownership, rights concerning family life, right to equality, right to life, protection from discrimination, freedom of religion, etc.

The basis of these rights does not depend only on a majority resolution. They are absolute rights given by God to mankind once and for all, expressed, among other places, in the Ten Commandments. Notice, that when Paul talks about authorities in Romans 13, he does so with reference to these very commands:

> Let no debt remain outstanding, except the continuing debt to love one another, for he who loves his fellow man has fulfilled the law. The commandments, "Do not commit adultery," "Do not murder," "Do not steal," "Do not covet," and whatever other commandment there may be, are summed up in this one rule: "Love your neighbor as yourself." Love does no harm to its neighbor. Therefore love is the fulfillment of the law (Rom 13:8-10).

It is in light of and in line with this that the authorities are to operate.

When a government, whether it be dictatorial or democratic, turns against God's commandments and principles for human life in its exercise of power, it has overstepped its powers and become a destructive force in society.

External Force

When the authorities carry out their commission correctly, they *hold no terror for those who do right, but for those who do wrong* (Rom 13:3). This means that through legislation and the application of external force they effectively stop corruption and crime. In order to do this, they have received permission from God to use force, that is, the sword.

> For he does not bear the sword for nothing. He is God's servant, an agent of wrath to bring punishment on the wrongdoer (Rom 13:4).

Though the language may sound somewhat old-fashioned, its implications are quite straightforward. Every citizen agrees instinctively with what this verse says. The authorities should have the external force necessary to prevent crime and maintain law and order within society, so that citizens can live without fear for life or property.

For this reason, the state has a certain amount of power with which to back up its words. But if the state is not founded on the Word of God and fails to adhere to its task, a real danger arises. The God-given institution of government can then be demoralized through power-abusers, who promote an anti-Christian social system to such an extent that the institution itself begins to oppose God. This can happen in either a dictatorial or a democratic system.

The Demoralization of Democracy

When governing authorities and their laws move away from original Christian values and roots, an opening is made which invites destructive forces to lead a country into eventual chaos. When a government begins to hold terror for those who do what is right, and begins to use its power to hinder the spreading of the Gospel, for example, or to legislate in direct opposition to Christian convictions, it is time to sound the alarm.

Such a trend places the country in jeopardy. The foundation of democracy is freedom, and a democratic society must, therefore, carefully guard its freedoms and privileges. If it exceed its limits or becomes apathetic, it invites every kind of misery.

Democracy is not merely a form of majority rule that arbitrarily sets 51% of the people against the other 49%. There are certain eternal principles that cannot be put to a ballot. Murder will never be right, even if a majority of 85% were to vote in its favor. A democracy is really only a democracy when its fundamental principles are protected. These very principles are responsible for the origin and existence of democracy.

If the fundamental principles upon which democracy is founded are erased through legislation, through a majority vote or current popular opinion, then democracy will soon no longer exist. Short-sighted egotism and questionable election tactics breed a rule of the street in which ungodliness is lawful and righteousness unlawful. This is the demoralization of democracy.

There are Limits

We must observe the laws of the government as it stands in authority over us. Romans 13:1 says, *Everyone must submit himself to the governing authorities.* Every Christian is familiar with this verse. We have little difficulty submitting to our Lord and Savior, Jesus Christ, and, therefore, should have no difficulty submitting to our authorities and obeying the law.

It is not primarily among Christians that one finds cases of deliberate offense, false tax declarations, undeclared earnings and other kinds of deceit. Romans 13:7 tells us that we should give to everyone what we owe them. *If you owe taxes, pay taxes,* the Bible says.

The government is entitled to certain things, which we are obliged to give them. At the same time, there are other things to which the state is not entitled; and we should not surrender these rights. When the state oversteps its authority in its exercise of power, it is time to protest and bring about change.

Several Pharisees came to trap Jesus by asking Him, *Is it right to pay taxes to Caesar or not?* (Matt 22:17). In other words, "What is our relationship with the state to be like?" Jesus took a coin that was engraved with Caesar's portrait and answered them by saying, *Give to Caesar what is Caesar's, and to God what is God's* (v. 21).

Jesus' response is extremely significant. It implies that there are certain things that belong to Caesar, or the government, and these can be rightfully claimed by the authorities. It also implies that there are things to which the government is not entitled.

We owe our government:
a) Taxes
b) A respectable lifestyle
c) Active and committed citizenship

We owe God:
a) Our full devotion and love
b) Our loyalty and obedience

If our authorities work in accordance with the principles that God has prescribed, there need be no conflict. But if they begin to demand loyalty and obedience in areas that are not under their jurisdiction, a conflict arises. This conflict can become so serious that it forces the believer to become a lawbreaker to keep a higher law—the law of God.

If the government attempts to forbid us from acting as the Word of God, the Bible, commands us, we must protest and refuse to obey. On the other hand, if the authorities command us to do something that the Word of God forbids, we again must become disobedient, in order to be obedient to the higher law of God. Every one of us, whether governing authorities or average citizens will be judged according to God's law, when the time comes for us to stand before Him.

The Bible is full of examples of ordinary people who found themselves in such a situation and chose to stand up for God.

The State is not God

In Daniel 3:17-18, King Nebuchadnezzar commanded three Hebrew men to worship his statue. This type of idolatry had been decreed through legislation and people were expected to worship on command. But Shadrach, Meshach and Abednego refused. Not an ounce of compromise was found in them, even though the penalty that awaited them was death.

Though they were cast into the fiery furnace, God was with them and they came out alive. Not a hair on their heads was singed, nor was the smell of smoke on their clothes. God's approval was upon them because they had dared to go against the majority and stand for what was right, in spite of the cost.

In Daniel 6:5-10, King Darius made a similar ruling by commanding people to worship him. Daniel refused and continued to pray as usual, to his God. He was cast into the den of lions and God rescued him.

From these two examples we see two principles emerge. First, the state, or those in authority, always tend toward pride and the abuse of power and a desire to be praised, honored and worshiped. Second, the state can easily present itself as a type of god that sets itself up to be the savior of mankind. However, this is not true and it will never be so.

In Daniel 4:30 the Babylonian king Nebuchadnezzar says, *Is not this the great Babylon **I** have built as the royal residence, by **my** mighty power and for the glory of **my** majesty?* His proud and dictatorial attitude demonstrated that self-exaltation was the true motivation behind his political and social projects. This is completely unacceptable to God.

The authorities are God's servants to carry out His will, and their authority comes from Him alone. Nebuchadnezzar's abuse of authority and independence in relation to God, meant his fall from power.

Authority Comes from God

When Pilate threatened Jesus by saying he had the ability to take life, Jesus replied, *You would have no power over me if it were not given to you from above* (John 19:11). Whatever power the authorities have has been given to them by a greater authority. And He will judge them if they misuse it and apply it to the wrong purposes, or take personal glory and command worship of themselves rather than worshiping Him who gave them power.

In Acts 12:21-23, Herod delivered a public address to the people. They began to exalt him as a god, and receiving this worship became his downfall. An angel of the Lord struck him and he died. In other words, the government that begins to exalt itself has embarked on a journey to its own destruction.

Could this happen today? The danger is obviously more likely under a dictatorship. Not long ago Mao Tse'tung was considered a divinity. The exaltation of Lenin in the former Soviet Union gave him divine attributes and the cult that surrounded him engaged in nothing short of adoration.

But this tendency exists even in a democratic society. The danger arises when the state begins to overstep its boundaries by doing more than it is meant to do. Luther defined a god as, "the one from whom you always expect every good thing and whom you trust and worship." In this sense, the state can indeed begin to take God's place.

It can eventually assume the role of "Big Brother", wanting to influence every area of every citizen's life. The state becomes omnipresent, all-powerful and omniscient. It takes the position of initiative-taker, educator, economist, journalist, banker, parent, supervisor, doctor, provider, etc. Eventually, citizens lose their independence altogether, being fully dependent on the state for everything.

This condition often creeps into a country. Its citizens become falsely reliant on a government that acts as a guardian, and wrongly independent of God—the only one who is able to help each individual with his or her problems.

Unchallenged, the state's guardianship becomes so all-encompassing that the individual becomes completely passive. Not one area of life escapes the control of the state. Our state-owned television stations dictate our opinion on every issue from spy submarines to AIDS, and we are without access to other sources of information that might help correct the picture given to us.

When a person is in this type of situation it seems strange to read international newspapers and discover that the commentary on world events is taken from an entirely different perspective. We quickly learn that the flow of information within our society is consciously steered to create a uniformity of opinion.

We Must Obey God

There are several examples in the New Testament where the disciples refused to follow the commands of the government. In Acts 5:28-29, the authorities had forbidden Peter and other disciples from teaching in the Name of Jesus, that is from preaching the Gospel. When asked why they persisted in doing so, Peter replied, *We must obey God rather than men!*

In other words, we are to obey other people and our authorities, but when they attempt to stop Christian gatherings and the furtherance of the Gospel, or if they try to prevent a believer from following God's commands, we must choose to obey God rather than man.

In Exodus 1:15-17, Pharaoh, the ruler then, decreed that the midwives were to kill every Hebrew male infant at birth. However, the midwives refused and were disobedient, since the right to life was a higher decree. As a result, God was kind to the midwives and let His blessing come over them (vv. 20-21).

Whenever people have been forced to break the law to obey the Word of God—when they have been forced, not when they have done so in rebellion—God's blessing has been upon them. Shadrach, Meshach and Abednego were preserved. Daniel's life was spared. Peter was protected. The midwives in Egypt were blessed.

God wants His people to be unafraid to stand up for what is right, even when it seems inopportune, when it goes against current popular opinion, or is resisted by the authorities.

Spiritual Weapons—Not Rebellion

Our obligation toward the authorities ends when they violate our right to follow God, but at the same time, outward rebellion is not God's plan. Believers have better weapons; spiritual weapons that are mighty to the pulling down of strongholds that rise up against the knowledge of God (2 Cor 10:3-5).

Jesus did not rebel as He stood before Pilate, but He won the battle anyway! When Paul was before Agrippa, he did not act in rebellion or take up arms—and he also won. Today, few people know who Agrippa was, but Paul's letters continue to affect the entire world.

Paul never used force, but people were able to say of him,

> "These men who have caused trouble all over the world have now come here. They are all defying Caesar's decrees, saying that there is another king, one called Jesus." When they heard this, the crowd and the city officials were thrown into turmoil (Acts 17:6-8).

3

The Church in Relation to the Authorities

Just as God has designed authorities to fulfill certain functions in the world, so too has He designed the Church. Our governing authorities uphold earthly law and order and have forcible means at their disposal. Similarly, the Church upholds spiritual law and order and has spiritual force at its disposal.

In Matthew 16:17-19 Jesus says:

> Blessed are you, Simon son of Jonah, for this was not revealed to you by man, but by my Father in heaven. And I tell you that you are Peter, and on this rock I will build my church, and the gates of Hades will not overcome it. I will give you the keys of the kingdom of heaven; whatever you bind on earth will be bound in heaven, and whatever you loose on earth will be loosed in heaven.

The Church is founded on the revelation that Jesus Christ is Messiah and Lord. He is over and above everything. This revelation is the living Word of God from heaven upon which the Church is built and the gates of hell are unable to stop it.

God has raised up the Body of Christ, the Church, to be a spiritual force without equal in this world. Its task is to shake the gates of hell and expand the Kingdom of God. We are to preach the Gospel of Jesus Christ and take as many people as we possibly can to heaven.

Confrontation

When we do what Jesus has commanded us, when we *go and make disciples of all nations* (Matt 28:19), there is bound to be confrontation. The Bible reveals that there are two different kingdoms, or families, in this world. These are the Kingdom of God and the kingdom of the devil (see Col 1:13), or the family of God and the family of the devil (see 1 John 3:8-10).

Many Christian leaders have tried to tone down this truth to avoid offending the rest of the world, while others have completely rejected it. However, Jesus and the Bible are very clear on this point. Every human being is created by God, but this does not automatically imply that everyone is a member of His family.

You must be born again to be part of God's Kingdom, or His family (John 3:3). This is not done through occasionally attending a church service or by having conservative values. You must personally realize that you are a sinner who is on the way to hell and in desperate need of help, rescue and salvation. You are unable to save yourself, but God has provided you with help and salvation, through the death of Jesus on the cross.

Your so-called good works are not good enough to pay the debt you have before God. For this reason, He placed all of your sins, shortcomings, failures and guilt on Jesus, who took it on Himself and died for your sake on Calvary. He took your sin, along with its many consequences, and paid your debt.

To become a part of God's family, you must admit that you are in need of help and realize that Jesus died for you. As you cry out to Him for help and confess Him as your personal Lord and Savior, you will be saved (Rom 10:9-10). The Spirit of God will then come into you, recreating your inner man and making you a new person altogether.

> Therefore, if anyone is in Christ, he is a new creation; the old has gone, the new has come! (2 Cor 5:17).

You are a new creation. The life of God has filled you and you are born again. The Spirit of God is also called the spirit of sonship (see Rom 8:15-17). He confirms within you that you are a child of God, a member of His family, with access to an abundant life and to every one of God's promises through faith in Jesus (see 2 Cor 1:20; John 16:24).

This is the way an individual becomes a member of the Body of Christ and a part of the family of God; the blood of Jesus cleanses from all sin and the Spirit of God gives new birth. You are transferred from the kingdom of darkness into citizenship in the Kingdom of God (Col 1:13).

People are not citizens of God's Kingdom simply because they are created by God and happen to find the Sermon on the Mount stimulating and interesting, or because they attend church on Advent Sunday and at Christmas. No, people must first be born again!

It is crucial that we understand that there are two kingdoms in the world, which are in direct opposition to one another. Spiritual leaders without the courage to teach what Jesus says on this issue, have no place in the pulpit. They do nothing but lead people astray and present them with false hopes. A Christian heritage will not help anyone get to heaven!

You can have many religious opinions or rituals, but unless your heart is changed and recreated, you are on the road to a lost eternity. The teaching that infant baptism and confirmation are sufficient for salvation, leads people to eternal destruction, if there is no accompanying Gospel of reconciliation, nor any help for the individual to be born again.

The Task of the Church

The Word of God calls the devil, "the prince of this world" (John 14:30). Jesus' task was to defeat him (Col 2:15; Luke 11:18-22) and free those who were held captive under his lordship. This struggle was decided through the victory that Jesus won, when He died on the cross and rose again on the third day.

In Revelation 1:18 Jesus declares, *I am the Living One; I was dead, and behold I am alive for ever and ever! And I hold the keys of death and Hades.* Jesus defeated the prince of this world and now He holds the keys to his kingdom. He has given these keys to His Church. As believers, we have been given the task of applying Jesus' victory in this world.

> Go into all the world and preach the good news to all creation. Whoever believes and is baptized will be saved, but whoever does not believe will be condemned. And these signs will accompany those who believe: In my name they will drive out demons; they will speak in new tongues; they will pick up snakes with their hands; and when they drink deadly poison, it will not hurt them at all; they will place their hands on sick people, and they will get well. After the Lord Jesus had spoken to them, he was taken up into heaven and

he sat at the right hand of God. Then the disciples went out and preached everywhere, and the Lord worked with them and confirmed his word by signs that accompanied it (Mark 16:15-20).

The Church should proclaim the victory of Jesus, preach the Gospel of freedom to the captives and forgiveness, salvation, healing and deliverance for all those who receive Him. When the Church preaches the Gospel to the world, people are given the opportunity to be saved. They receive hope and their lives can be changed. The power of God can transform even the most desperate situations.

Through the Gospel, people are able to experience that God is alive, that He really speaks with them, and that He is willing and able to work miracles because of His love for them. People are God's creation. He paid a tremendous price—His only Son—to regain their fellowship.

A church that backslides and fails to boldly proclaim the Kingdom of God and salvation, has completely lost its purpose and meaning. It has become nothing more than a religious organization in the midst of all the others. Its salt has been lost. Tragically, this is quite common.

The battle between the kingdom of darkness and the Kingdom of God involves an attempt on behalf of the devil to infiltrate the Church, so that it loses its power, its boldness and its purpose. Through worldliness, cowardice, compromise and a wrong desire to please men, the Gospel has been diluted and becomes a series of platitudes that serves only to whitewash graves rather than to wake up the lost to salvation.

The Church has been ashamed of God's Word. It has criticized God's Word and torn it apart rather than preached it with boldness, so that men and women could be affected by the Gospel, repent and be saved. The fear of calling sin what it really is and of purging sinful behavior, has filled the Church with impurity and taken away its power of resistance against the world.

Rather than expanding the Kingdom of God, the Church has mimicked the world and been robbed of the power and presence of God. Praise God, however, those days are gone.

An Operational Church

The Church is once again standing up and occupying its rightful place. Believers are shaking off their sin, worldliness, doubt and unbelief. They are beginning to believe that God is actually who He says He is in His Word, and that He is willing and able to do exactly what He says. This awakening implies an inevitable confrontation in the spiritual realm.

If the devil cannot pacify the Church and put it to sleep with worldliness, or cajole it into compromise and denial, he will threaten it, yelling and screaming, lying and ridiculing, in an attempt to scare it into silence. But it is too late. The Body of Christ is already rising up to take its position in the earth.

The Church is called to expand the Kingdom of God and to command a position of rulership in the spiritual realm. It has four primary functions:

1. **To preach** the full Gospel to the world, allowing God to confirm His Word with signs and wonders so that people can be saved and helped.

2. **To feed** the sheep, giving believers food from the Word of God that enables them to grow spiritually strong and become all that God desires them to be.

3. **To rule** in the realm of the spirit so that the spiritual forces of evil in the heavenly realms (Eph 6:12) have no advantage over a country and cannot lead people into destruction.

4. **To prophesy** to the authorities and the government, enabling them to know the will of God and lead the country correctly.

By carrying out these tasks, the Church is serving others, people's needs are met and God is glorified.

Let's examine the last two points mentioned above.

We need to understand that God has given the Church an authoritative function in the earth. However, its means of rulership is different to that of political rule. We are not called to preach politics, although God has something to say about every area of life. There is not an area in which God does not want His Kingdom to expand and where He does not want to help and bless.

God created man with a mandate to rule over creation (see Gen 1:26-28; Ps 8:6-9). This position of authority was lost through the Fall, but has once again been regained through Christ. By being born again we are made a part of the Body of Christ, and consequently we have become seated with Him in the heavenly realms (see Eph 2:6).

We Do Not Battle Against People

Ephesians 1:20-23 tells us that the Church, or the Body of Christ, is situated above every spiritual principality and power. God uses the Church to demonstrate Jesus' victory, and the devil's ultimate defeat, to the rulers and authorities in the heavenly realms (see Eph 3:10). In other words, the Church has been given authority to break down and destroy the demonic strongholds that the devil has built in the spiritual realm to corrupt and destroy people and their nations:

> The weapons we fight with are not the weapons of the world. On the contrary, they have divine power to demolish strongholds. We demolish arguments and every pretension that sets itself up against the knowledge of God, and we take captive every thought to make it obedient to Christ (2 Cor 10:4-5).

There is a battle taking place in the spiritual realm, a battle over the eternal destiny of people and nations. The Bible is very clear on this point. Jesus Himself often talked about it. This idea may seem foreign and even frightening to the secular mind, but it is a basic (though often neglected) Bible teaching with which believers have been familiar throughout history.

The battle is not physical, nor is it against people:

> For our struggle is not against flesh and blood, but against the rulers, against the authorities, against the powers of this dark world and against the spiritual forces of evil in the heavenly realms (Eph 6:12).

Our battle is not a physical one, neither are our weapons physical weapons. Second Corinthians 10:4-5 tells us that the weapons of our warfare are not carnal, or physical. They are spiritual weapons— and they are powerful and effective. Our primary weapons are:

a) The Word of God
b) And prayer

When the prophet Elijah prayed (Jas 5:16-18), the entire nation was affected. It is time that this type of prayer returned. When Jesus prayed and taught the Word, people marveled and said, *What is this? A new teaching—and with authority! He even gives orders to evil spirits and they obey him* (Mark 1:27). The time has also come for our preaching to regain this type of authority.

The Bible has much to say regarding the Church's position of power and its authority and dominance. Many people have misunderstood this and some have even slandered it with ill intent. We are not talking about misusing other people or using political power. Jesus said, *My kingdom is not of this world* (John 18:36), but He did not mean that His Kingdom had nothing to do with the world.

On the contrary, God's Kingdom is closely linked to this world, although the Kingdom of God and His Church do not operate as the world does. The spiritual authority Jesus possessed was far greater than the religious and political power of the Pharisees, or of Herod and Pontius Pilate.

Jesus healed the ear that Peter had cut off when using a weapon to defend Him. Spiritual defense is far superior. When Peter was thrown in prison for preaching the Gospel, the Church prayed and an angel opened the doors of the jail. Not even the armed guards could prevent this from happening.

The spiritual forces and resources available to us have the potential to change a country. They are much greater and more effective than the external social, economical and political resources the world has at its disposal.

A Blessing for the Country

The Church must take its place and fulfill its commission so that it then becomes a protective force within society and a blessing to the entire nation. The devil begins to destroy a country by secularizing the Church so that it backslides and cannot fulfill its protective role in society.

As Christians we can be quick to complain about situations within the community that we are unhappy about, not realizing that the blame for much of the misery we see lies directly with us. If the Church had maintained its position of dominion and refused to compromise with sin, our nations would have avoided much misfortune.

Yet when Church leaders stand up to defend ungodliness, they release destruction throughout their country. The keys to our power are then thrown into the devil's hands (Matt 16:19). The Church, then, actually releases sin and binds up righteousness rather than doing the opposite. This is terribly serious!

In Matthew 16:18 Jesus tells us that *the gates of Hades will not overcome the Church*. At that time, a gate was the place where the elders of the town ruled, advised and carried out judgment. A gate is, therefore, a picture of authority.

Jesus is showing us that Satan's kingdom, with all of its authority, cannot stand against the Church that firmly stands on the rock, on the revelation of God's Word. The living Word of God is our greatest asset. It is a hammer that destroys and a fire that consumes (see Jer 23:29).

God's Word is a sword that divides between soul and spirit, revealing what is in the heart of man (Heb 4:12). It has the supernatural ability to create, to heal, to restore and to completely transform. Without the Word of the Lord, a country is lost, but with His Word it is mightily blessed. As Jeremiah says, *O land, land, land, hear the word of the Lord* (Jer 22:29).

Prophesy!

The Church does not only hold a position of authority and dominion in the spirit world, its task is to speak prophetically to the governing authorities. The Church and the government have two very different tasks. The authorities are ordained by God to lead in political issues; a commission which the Church has not been given.

This by no means implies that believers themselves cannot be politicians. They most certainly can, and they are of great benefit in such a position. The more true believers we have as politicians, the better.

However, the task of the Church is spiritual and not primarily political. Nevertheless, this task includes prophesying to the authorities. If the Church fails to faithfully and powerfully preach God's Word to the nation, the country is without the direction, leading and correction it needs. The Church must carry out this task without retreating from opposition or from the risk of unpopularity and false accusation.

Unless the authorities hear the Word of the Lord, they cannot administer justice; and the Church itself will be the first to suffer as its freedom begins to disappear. An entire country will inevitably experience the consequences of a government that works against God's laws. If the Church does not react, judgment will eventually overtake it.

> The Lord has a charge to bring against you that live in the land: There is no faithfulness, no love, no acknowledgment of God in the land (Hos 4:1).

The land was found lacking in three areas:

a) Truth—there was deceit, deception and manipulation.

b) Love—there was no love for those who needed it.

c) Acknowledgment of God—the Word of God was not considered in everyday life.

This resulted in violence and immorality (v. 2), and the land and its produce wasted away. The people brought a curse on themselves that affected the entire country, both physically and economically.

Whose Fault is It?

Hosea goes on to talk about the reasons behind the country's problems and says, *Don't point your finger at someone else, and try to pass the blame to him! Look, priest, I am pointing my finger at you* (Hos 4:4, TLB).

What is meant by mentioning the priest? He was the spiritual leader with the task of delivering God's Word to the people.

Hosea 4:6 (TLB) says:

> My people are destroyed because they don't know me, and it is all your fault, you priests, for you yourselves refuse to know me! Therefore I refuse to recognize you as my priests. Since you have forgotten my laws, I will "forget" to bless your children.

The consequences of the leaders' rejection of the Word of God infiltrated the entire land.

Righteousness exalts a nation, but sin is a disgrace to any people (Prov 14:34).

When the righteousness that comes through faith in Jesus is preached, believed and applied, the whole nation is exalted. The preaching of the Word of God can change the atmosphere of an entire country.

Terrifying Consequences

If the Church fails to speak out, the government will begin to legislate irrevocable laws that conflict with the Word of God and will damage the country. One example is the abortion law, which clearly contradicts the commandment "you shall not murder".

How a government can expect a country to enjoy continued prosperity when it consciously takes the lives of thousands of unborn infants every year is incomprehensible. Yet they continue to be killed. Why? Because no one has consulted them!

Certainly no politician would have voted yes to abortion if he or she were the one lying in their mother's womb, waiting for the moment of birth and the beginning of life. The so-called "scientific" explanations of when a fetus actually becomes a human being are so meager and dishonest that hearing them makes one blush with embarrassment.

Seldom have lies exerted such control over science that it has become an institution of murder, as with the abortion issue. This is not to mention the latest addition to the abortion law, recently discussed in France, where their parliament debated the possibility of killing children up to four days after birth (yes, you read it correctly!), should they have serious birth defects.

One could go through the Ten Commandments (which is not my present intention) and demonstrate how laws have been passed that are in direct violation to each of them.

Freedom of Religion?

The Swedish law of 1951 which applies to the freedom of religion says in Paragraph 1: "Each and every individual possesses the right to freely practice his religion, provided he does not disturb the peace of society or cause general annoyance."

The natural question is, who decides what is meant by "disturbing the peace"? The believers themselves? Or an unfavorably disposed authority who can use a flexible paragraph to restrict the freedom of groups by which it feels threatened? Something that seems unlikely today may become a reality tomorrow, for which the Church is often completely unprepared.

Lawlessness

In Second Thessalonians 2:7 the expression "the secret power of lawlessness" is used. Paul is referring to the fact that the Antichrist, or "the man of lawlessness" (vv. 3,8) will appear in the last days. His arrival will not happen by accident. The stage must first be set for him.

Verse 7 says that there is something that must be removed that presently holds him back and hinders his appearance. But although he is unable to appear as yet, the "secret power of lawlessness" is already active and at work today.

In First John 4:3 we read about the "spirit of Antichrist" that is already in the world. What is this? It is an influence that draws mankind away from God and His Word, so that on many points His laws are disobeyed. By invalidating and amending government laws, one can unconsciously legislate a lawlessness that, in turn, breeds a generation of people who are highly receptive to the Antichrist when he eventually appears.

Standing in the way of this is the Church (2 Thess 2:6-7). "But the Church cannot stop the Antichrist," you might say! No, his time is coming; but the anti-Christian influence prior to his arrival can definitely be stopped, hindered and delayed.

However, if the Church fails to react to ungodly legislation and other occurrences because they fall into the category of "politics," then, through its own passivity, it serves to hasten a hateful, depraved and godless society with tremendous social and economic problems. The result of this negative change will be most felt by the Church itself.

We Can Do Something

In Genesis 19:9, the people of Sodom reacted fiercely to Lot, one of Abraham's relatives, even though Lot himself neither lived victoriously nor was especially holy. They said to him, *Get out of our way!* adding, *This fellow came here as an alien, and now he wants to play the judge!* The people of Sodom saw Lot as a judge. Why? Because his presence judged them!

Lot was not especially vocal, since the story shows us that he did not live in personal victory. However, he still suffered from the immorality and loose morals in the City of Sodom.

> He rescued Lot, a righteous man, who was distressed by the filthy lives of lawless men [for that righteous man, living among them day after day, was tormented in his righteous soul by the lawless deeds he saw and heard] (2 Pet 2:7-8).

Because Lot did not live like his fellow citizens, they saw him as judgmental and lacking in love. The same is true today. Many people living in gross sin and rampant ungodliness want "forgiveness and love" from the Church and a legislation that allows them to perpetuate their depraved lifestyle. However, that type of love is not love at all.

Preachers and church leaders who say that God tolerates everything because He is love, are not following God—-they are following the devil. Our God is a holy God and an all-consuming fire (see Heb 12:29).

God was unable to judge Sodom while Lot was there (see Gen 19:22). He had a hindering effect, both on sin and its judgment. The Church has the same effect today. Like Lot, we must live as strangers, refusing to follow the customs of the world and being unafraid of seeming judgmental.

God loves the sinner, but not the sin itself. There is help for every sinner who repents and forsakes his sin. The Church not only has a warning capacity, but a counseling one as well. The Bible is full of examples of people who held a position of authority and were a blessing to their country and their immediate surroundings.

Joseph is an example of such a man. He was exalted to a position second only to the Pharaoh of Egypt, and through this position he was able to save the lives of many people, by allowing them to obtain grain in a time of great famine. Even his own family was saved. Because of Joseph's position, Jacob and his sons lived in Egypt under Pharaoh's protection, and God's plan to make for Himself a covenant people continued unhindered.

Daniel is another example of a man who was placed in a position of authority. He was a government official under the reign of four kings: Nebuchadnezzar, Belshazzar, Darius and Cyrus. He served under a heathen government, but was able to keep himself free and pure. He refused to compromise. Instead, he spoke the Word of God to his rulers, giving them counsel from heaven that preserved them from complete catastrophe.

Esther is an example of godly leadership. She became queen to the Persian king Xerxes and because of her position she was able to save her people, the Jews, from extermination. Her uncle, Mordecai, reminded her of how important it was that she use her position to help her people, saying, *who knows but that you have come to royal position for such a time as this?* (Esth 4:14).

"Party Megaphones"

The believer's influence in political matters is greater than we think. God wants His people to be everywhere so that they can pray, bless, advise and bring the warnings that stop a country from going in the wrong direction. It is, therefore, remarkable that the Church has been asleep in this area. Churches have either politely accepted their state financial support and kept quiet, or they have been afraid of becoming too political.

Strangely enough, the accusations of wrong political involvement by the Church have often come from fellow Christians, who are themselves actively involved in politics. A terrible fear of a "Christian right wing" has been broadcast by those who are themselves noticeably left wing. During the past twenty years, these people have strongly undermined and infiltrated the Christian ranks with a combination of socialism and liberal "denial theology," both of which are far from Biblical Christianity.

This sort of influence has continued virtually unhindered within present-day Christianity. However, if someone dares raise a voice today in defense of the Gospel, the cry "right wing Christianity" is immediately heard in the other camp. This is somewhat embarrassing, especially when the individuals who make the most noise are themselves tied to, and in some cases salaried by, a left wing political party.

Right of Private Ownership

The prophet Nathan is another example of someone who spoke the Word of the Lord to a national leader. He prophesied against king David, the governing authority at that time. When David fell for Bathsheba, it was not only David as a private individual who fell, it was David as a man in authority.

David committed adultery with Bathsheba, and when she became pregnant he tried to cover-up his sin by bringing her husband Uriah home from the battlefront. However, Uriah refused to lie with his wife in order to obey the rules of war that prohibited it. This shows us that the authorities themselves must submit to the law and cannot merely act at their own discretion. David then sent Uriah back to the front and had him betrayed so the enemy could kill him.

David's plan was flawless—if it were not for God. God exists and He brings the shady dealings of politicians to the surface when He wants to do so.

If authorities overstep their borders, this must be exposed and unveiled. Otherwise their corruption will influence the destiny of an entire nation. God spoke to the prophet Nathan, who went to King David and told him a parable:

> The Lord sent Nathan to David. When he came to him, he said, "There were two men in a certain town, one rich and the other poor. The rich man had a very large number of sheep and cattle, but the poor man had nothing except one little ewe lamb he had bought. He raised it, and it grew up with him and his children. It shared his food, drank from his cup and even slept in his arms. It was like a daughter to him. Now a traveler came to the rich man, but the rich man refrained from taking one of his own sheep or cattle to prepare a meal for the traveler who had come to him. Instead, he took the ewe lamb that belonged to the poor man and prepared it for the one who had come to him." David burned with anger against the man and said to Nathan, "As surely as the Lord lives, the man who did this deserves to die! He must pay for that lamb four times over, because he did such a thing and had no pity." Then Nathan said to David, "You are the man!" (2 Sam 12:1-7)

What sort of comparison is Nathan making? Bathsheba is likened to the lamb that the poor man owned. On the one hand we see what happened in the area of private morality—that David committed adultery with Bathsheba, something that was wrong and shameful. But we also see the ruler David, who unlawfully seized something that did not belong to him; the lamb was the private possession of an individual citizen.

This brings us to another side of the issue. God reacts unfavorably toward authorities who begin to take possession of people's private belongings, based on their own lust for power and selfish desires—even if these desires are disguised with attractive phrases and a variety of ideologies.

The commandment, *You shall not commit adultery* is not to be broken. Nor is the commandment, *You shall not steal* or, *You shall not covet your neighbor's house...*or *anything that belongs to your neighbor,* to be violated.

God always has been, and always will be, a protector of private property. He is not in favor of selfishness, but He does support our right to ownership. Selfishness can exist on both a state and an individual level. God responds negatively to a government that has an ideology that weakens or attacks the right of private ownership.

At that point, the state has gone far beyond its God-given powers and has become the people's predator. Then it is time for the prophet Nathan to come forth and rebuke its greed and lust for power.

4

The Breakdown of Socialism

A person is a product of what he thinks. Whatever occupies him internally will color him externally. The foundations of a person's life are laid through thoughts, concepts and ideologies. This foundation will influence his attitudes and actions for the rest of his life—if nothing happens to radically change his personal philosophy. For this reason, the mind, which is the arena of thought and creativity, is a battleground in our lives.

> We demolish arguments and every pretension that sets itself up against the knowledge of God, and we take captive every thought to make it obedient to Christ (2 Cor 10:5).

Here Paul mentions several different concepts, including "arguments," "pretensions" and "thoughts." In verse 4 he also calls them strongholds.

What are strongholds? They are thoughts, ideas or ideologies (a systematic construction of thoughts) that are built up to become a stronghold in one's personality. They are houses (mental "strongholds") of thoughts that influence people and exercise control in their lives. In verse 4, Paul writes that we have been given spiritual weapons that can break down these strongholds.

But why do they need to be broken down? Because they "raise themselves up against the knowledge of

God." Certain thoughts and ideas actively raise themselves up against God's thoughts, or against the knowledge of God. These ideologies are designed to occupy a person's mind so that he or she has difficulty receiving God's Word—the thoughts and the revelation that come from God.

Romans 8:7 says, *the sinful mind is hostile to God. It does not submit to God's law, nor can it do so.* This refers to those thoughts and conceptions that are in rebellion to God's Word and God's laws. These thoughts and ideas do not originate with the Spirit of God (see Rom 8:5,7), but from a mind that is rebellious and resistant toward Him.

In Matthew 16:21-23, Jesus declared that He would go to Jerusalem, suffer and die, and on the third day rise again. Suddenly Peter *began to rebuke him* (v. 22); to which Jesus answered, *Get behind me, Satan! You are a stumbling block to me; you do not have in mind the things of God, but the things of men.*

Jesus responded quite drastically here. He understood that Peter was speaking the thoughts and plans of Satan that were designed to stop God's plan to redeem and save mankind, were Jesus to accept them. Peter himself wanted only the best for Jesus and was unaware of whose thoughts and ideas he was conveying, but Jesus saw beyond them.

Peter's thoughts were not from God, they were the thoughts of men, which, according to Jesus, were inspired by the devil. "Out of my sight, Satan!" Jesus said. Peter was not Satan, but his "human thoughts" were demonically inspired and were designed to prevent God's plan from becoming a reality. Such thoughts, therefore, had to be exposed and destroyed.

This account clearly demonstrates the way in which the mind is a battleground for foreign thoughts and ideologies. The thought patterns which take hold of a person's mind will pull him in a particular direction. Therefore, the thoughts and ideologies we accept, are extremely significant.

We are exhorted in Romans 12:2 to renew our minds and to no longer be conformed to the way of the world. As those who have been born again, *we have the mind of Christ* (1 Cor 2:16). We are actually able to think His thoughts.

Attractive Ideologies

All ideologies contain elements that are positive and correct, otherwise they would have little success. Every ideology appeals to a legitimate need or desire. They also have the ability to correctly relate a certain number of facts regarding the world around us. Millions of people would never receive or cherish these ideologies if this were not so.

At the same time, every ideology has a practical and a theoretical side. The practical element points to immediate needs and promises a change. The theoretical deals with the abstract; building a systematic, mental foundation for its actions.

When people encounter a new ideology, they seldom analyze in detail its fundamental ideas and dogmas. Instead, almost carelessly, they accept the practical program of action presented. Plans of action appeal to people's immediate needs and to their emotions.

In a political election, for example, many people are unable to define the different platforms of the various parties in question. They are more likely to vote out of routine or based on what they themselves stand to gain in issues such as child allowance, pensions, increased salaries, greater work opportunities, etc.

These direct products are extremely important, but the ideology that produces them is of far greater importance. Election promises are always attractive, but the real question is whether there are hidden snares, which will eventually lead in the wrong direction.

Do not Confuse the Concepts!

As we examine political ideologies, we must first recognize that, seen through God's eyes and according to His Word, a system that measures up to His standard is non-existent. On the other hand, there are political ideas that more or less correspond to His principles as expressed in the Ten Commandments.

Let's examine an ideology that is of particular relevance—socialism. Sweden is a socialist country. Outside the Eastern bloc, Sweden is probably the most socialistic country in Europe, much more so than its Scandinavian neighbors. Sweden has a long tradition of socialistic influence.

After several generations of this, the Swedish mind has become accustomed to thinking in a particular way, and it often reacts with surprise when other countries think and act differently. As a result of this long-term influence, the general populace has virtually lost all comparative ability.

People have grown used to terms such as "equality," "security" and "solidarity," words that represent important and meaningful concepts. They may warm us emotionally, but by whom are they actually defined? They may hold one connotation for one person, while denoting something completely different for another—entirely dependent on context and underlying ideology.

Using words like "community," "solidarity," and so on, means little if they are used in a context that clearly contradicts the Word of God, the Bible.

First, we must distinguish between socialism as a system of belief and that which social democratic governments have accomplished in Sweden and other countries during the course of history. This was especially the case at the turn of the century, when the government paid attention to the interests of underprivileged workers and gave them the right to a tolerable existence.

No one can deny that valuable contributions have been made which have raised people's standard of living. Nevertheless, the socialistic interpretation of existence and its methodology must be rejected. A desire for equality and social justice is not equivalent to socialism. Other parties possess as much, if not more, of this quality. Socialism has no patent on social reforms, in spite of what it would like to think.

A Socialistic Paradise

Whether expressed through so-called social democracy or through communism, the roots and objectives of socialism are the same. Existing differences lie only in their methods and procedures. The common goal is to reach a societal paradise, that is, a classless society, without help from God. In the socialist society, the state takes the place of God as the savior, provider and helper of mankind.

More precisely, socialism is built on an atheistic, anti-Christian and materialistic foundation. Its concept of man and society does not correspond in the slightest with the Bible, but stands in direct opposition to it.

According to socialism, matter has always existed. Because God does not exist, He has not created the world. Instead, it has developed through evolutionary, natural laws that automatically push its development forward. Among these laws are the class laws.

Mankind is divided into different classes that invariably struggle against one another. Finally, based on historical necessity, the working class will prevail and restore the classless, socialistic society. In the communist system, this shift of power takes place through revolution, and within social democracy, by means of parliamentary reforms. The overall goal, however, remains the same.

This interpretation of the class struggle must be rejected. Such a model can lead to a form of self-righteousness, so that everything that is disliked can be termed "bourgeois." That which is "bourgeois" is reactionary, and merely stands in the way of the restoration of the social system.

Religion, Christianity and the Church are put in this category and can only be tolerated if they are lacking in any significant influence within society. To ensure this, the Church is often put in a position of economic dependency on the state, with the government itself appointing its bishops and leaders. The Church is further controlled through the socialistically inspired, secularized theology, taught at the state universities.

Collectivism and the Guardianship Mentality

The socialistic view of man is anti-individualistic. Man is defined as a collective being whose worth is determined in relation to his work and the state. Because the individual has not been created by God, he lacks any real personal worth, even though one may speak warmly about the importance of the individual.

Therefore, the legal security of the individual is always at risk in a socialist society, as the individual is forced to conform to the collective system. The state and public sectors grow, while the individual is to an increasing degree controlled and steered from above. In Sweden, the average citizen is hardly able to put up a fence without first obtaining building permission.

This overall feeling that everything must be approved by superiors, infiltrates society until personal initiative is stolen. This form of collectivism leads to listlessness, lack of initiative, and finally to irresponsibility and moral breakdown. People grow apathetic rather than becoming more responsible. Initiative is treated with suspicion rather than encouraged, and no one dares to elevate himself above the crowd.

Monopolization also thrives in this kind of society. The state acquires all of the vital workings of the community, especially within the financial sphere. According to socialism, capital and private ownership are bad. Therefore, all forms of socialism are fundamentally opposed to private ownership and desire to transfer as much as possible to the state, thus increasing the size of the public sector.

However, according to the Bible, private ownership is not at all wrong (see Ex 20:15,17; Eph 4:28). Two of the Ten Commandments, in fact, specifically defend the right to own private property.

Socialistic tax legislation lays extremely high taxes on the citizen and is a direct consequence of this train of thought. Financial resources, it is thought, should belong to the state, which has the right to distribute people's money.

Taxation is Biblical (see Rom 13:6-7), but not when based on the misconception that the ownership of private property is wrong and should somehow be penalized. The Bible warns those who are rich and urges them to give generously (see 1 Tim 6:17-18; Jas 5:4-5) and to pay their employees well. However, it does not say that the possessions of the citizens belong to the state or that the state has the authority to self-elect to redistribute them.

Conformity of Thought

The tendency toward monopoly applies not only to national economy and economic planning—more than anything else it applies to people's opinions. Conformity of thought exerts an incredible influence in a socialistic society. The mass media, primarily radio and television, are monopolized, causing the flow of information and the presentation of facts to follow a prescribed pattern. Anything disturbing the socialistic society is angled, distorted or quietened, allowing the monopoly to effectively control all available information.

Within every socialistic society there is strong resistance to releasing the monopoly over both the mass media and public education. The educational system is a vital factor in the socialist society, in its ability to indoctrinate and streamline the masses according to the wishes of the state. Private or independent schools are therefore opposed, often through state-induced financial starvation.

Socialism fails to recognize that parents have the primary responsibility, or even the right to bring up their children according to their individual convictions. The state prefers to direct upbringing and to begin this process as quickly as possible.

For a mother to choose to stay home with her children is virtually considered improper. The system of taxation and salary levels more or less force her back into the working world, even though she would prefer to stay at home. As a result, the authorities assume the child's upbringing.

The basis of legislation in favor of family rights lies in the commandment *honor your father and your mother* (Ex 20:12). This right is badly undermined in a socialistic society.

International Socialistic Solidarity

Another danger zone within socialism is the view it holds called "internationalism." The majority of democratic ideologies are, or at least ought to be, involved in bringing justice and help to those in distress around the world. The Biblical view of man is free from prejudices that are based on race, sex, ideology or religion. Every country ought to be involved in the needs of other nations. Giving has always been central to Christianity.

The Bible speaks clearly about the individuality of nations and their right to maintain this (see Acts 17:26; Matt 25:32). Throughout history there have emerged distorted forms of nationalism, in which one nation has risen up against others and claimed to be superior. This sort of nationalism is wrong and dangerous. Germany under Hitler's rule, and Italy under Mussolini exemplify this.

However, there also exists a true, sound patriotism that involves being thankful and proud of one's country, taking responsibility for its well-being, and carrying out the duties of citizenship in national loyalty.

Socialism, though, invokes a different type of solidarity that is produced by the so-called "international proletariat;" that is, socialistic proletarians around the world waiting to unite. For the Moscow-based communist party, solidarity toward one's own country does not matter; what counts is solidarity with international socialism. This is reflected in a number of ways.

When such a party comes to power, their program always includes a reduction in military spending and criticism of any increase in this area. One can wonder if this stance is based on general idealism or on solidarity toward powers that are outside the country itself. It is especially suspicious when one knows that the socialistic dogmas themselves support violence and the takeover of political power through revolutionary means.

In Sweden, for instance, coastal sightings of reconnaissance submarines have been reported within the past year. Therefore, it is remarkable, to say the least, that a well-known representative for the left wing communist party (VPK), claimed in the national press and on television that the military had fabricated the sightings in order to raise the level of defense spending.

It is also interesting to note that through the presence of VPK in parliament (at just over 4%), the social democrats are able to maintain a majority seating. It is well-known that many social democrats vote for the communist party simply to keep it in parliament, knowing their dire need of the party to maintain their own power and to bring about the social Utopia they have as their goal.

A party with blatantly non-democratic tendencies, both in background and in purpose, is the party that currently has a decisive influence on the future of Sweden.

Development aid from Sweden is necessary and justified, but it should not go exclusively to socialistic countries where there is often a meager understanding of democracy and a dictator who adheres to the pattern of socialism. In addition, there is often open persecution of Christians and dissidents in the countries to which Sweden sends its aid.

Lust for Power

Every normal human being wants a life of peace, justice, equality and security. It is important to understand that these words do not belong exclusively to any one ideology. These concepts are not in themselves socialistic. A socialist does not have a monopoly on the use or definition of these concepts.

Democracy is another word that has been abused and distorted. The words "democracy and "socialism" have become virtually interchangeable in Sweden, though the truth is that in whatever part of the world socialistic ideas have appeared, the direct opposite has been achieved. There has either been a serious reduction or a complete abolition of democracy.

The purpose of this book is not to catalog or complain about existing problems in Sweden, or in any other country for that matter, which have been caused by the exercise of socialistic power. There are others who have greater insight and ability in this area than myself. However, each of us must see clearly the nature and spirit of socialism; its origin and roots and its real purpose.

As a political system, socialism is riddled with problems the world over. Many consider it outdated and old-fashioned. In many places, Sweden included, socialism stands as a greying representative of power, with its guardianship mentality and bureaucratic inability to solve problems effectively. With its incorrect view of man and society, socialism does not have the power to accomplish what it promises.

In reality, people simply do not function in the way the socialistic world view would like to think. This explains the mysterious disappearance of governmental spies, the collapse in the educational system, and the increased incidence of tax evasion. In spite of all the nice-sounding slogans, reality is a very different picture from the one painted by the socialists.

Tragically, those who stand in positions of authority are themselves all too aware of this. With their idealism long ago destroyed, all that remains for them is to try to stay in power.

Those who have been caught up in the system become its greatest critics. The general populace has long ago seen its emptiness. The individual cannot be put to one side indefinitely, especially when he begins to realize that socialism poses a real threat to his personal integrity and the rights of the family. It threatens private ownership and even national integrity itself. If the submarine sightings continue, it will not be long before people begin to put two and two together and start to react.

A Negative Influence

In its deepest sense, socialism is not just an ideology. Its nature is fundamentally spiritual. The Bible clearly says that the devil utilizes mental strongholds in order to raise them up against the knowledge of God and stop His influence in people's thoughts and lives.

A system of thought that openly denies the existence of God, embraces rebellion against His system of order, transgresses His laws on one point after another, and attempts to produce what He has promised but without His help, has by no means received its inspiration from God.

Where then has its inspiration come from? We know that it has not been inspired by God. On the contrary, socialism in its many forms has always been known to actively resist God. Marx hardly received his ideas from the Bible. Lenin was by no means inspired by Jesus.

Branting, Wigforss and other well-known Swedish Social Democrats clearly dissociated themselves from many of the fundamental Christian doctrines. Where does their inspiration come from, then? According to the Bible, only one other possible source exists.

There is violent confrontation between ideologies in this day and age. Behind it is a battle in the spiritual realm. We live at a time when Jesus' return is imminent. The strongholds that have been raised against Him, to hold people away from Him, will be crushed. A revival is on the way that will change the spiritual atmosphere of the nation of Sweden.

However, before this can happen the heaviness that lies over the people like a lid, stealing their initiative and making them generally passive and apathetic, must be removed. This bondage is not from people or ideologies, but from spiritual beings. The people who actually represent these ideologies are often unconscious of this struggle. They are merely deceived and taken advantage of.

The battle is never against "flesh and blood," but against spiritual principalities and powers, according to Ephesians 6:12. Using the prayer of faith and the preaching of the Word of God, the Church has been given the authority to bind and defeat these powers. An entire nation can then be free from the negative influences that have held it captive.

5

Humanism's Dilemma

Another ideology that has infiltrated the minds of most people today is humanism. Although the word creates a positive first impression, in general we are not fully aware of what it represents.

When we talk about humanism and its influence on people's minds, we are not talking about the concept of "human" (referring to mankind) or the "humanities" (meaning the philosophical, historical and linguistic areas of study). We are referring to humanism—the system of thought that denies God's existence and sovereignty and places man at the center of everything, making all things relative.

Humanism's Roots

Humanism has its roots in the Renaissance period and even prior to that, when the expression "Man—the measure of everything" was coined. A stiff, superstitious, scholastic and often unbiblical theology, together with the authoritarian church of the Middle Ages, helped prepare the ground for the Renaissance.

During the Renaissance, the fine arts blossomed and people felt stimulated afresh, as though they had thrown aside the inhibitions that had hindered their creativity. This in itself was not negative.

Man has been created by God and has been given an incredible creative ability, something the Church has occasionally failed to understand. In terms of ideology, however, the "baby was thrown out with the bath water" and instead of God, man becomes his own starting point.

During the Age of Enlightenment, when work within the sciences began, this tendency grew into a form of rationalism that increasingly denied and questioned the supernatural. If man's intellect and careful research failed to explain God, and if his experimentation was unable to find Him, then surely God could not exist. Such was the line of thinking that emerged.

Enthusiasm over scientific progress became so great that God was no longer needed in order to understand or manage the world. During this period, the Bible was attacked and criticized, based on so-called "scientific postulation." Everything that could not be understood or experienced empirically was simply rejected. The neologism of the 1700s was the beginning of all Biblical criticism to follow.

During the 1800s, Darwin's theory of evolution and socialism's analysis of society exerted the primary influence on thought. As we approach the 1900s, we find Freud's psychoanalysis and existentialism becoming significant influences. These components and several others have blended to form what we commonly term "humanism."

Biblical Foundations

In short, what happened as a result of these developments was the undermining and disappearance of three foundational Biblical principles:

1. That God really is an objective reality.
2. That what He says is objective truth with eternal application.

3. That He moves and acts in human history.

This view of life has been the basis of traditional Christianity throughout the ages and has strongly influenced our society. People have believed in God and have applied the belief that God is a real, personal and living God, in their everyday situations.

God exists. He is not just an opinion, ideology or system of thought; He is real. Because He is an objective reality, He is able to communicate with His creation. He speaks through His Word. God is true. Therefore, His Words are true and they provide an objective foundation for understanding the world around us. What He says in His Word is of universal application and eternal significance.

Christians have always believed this, and they still do. These views have affected society's world view, not to mention its laws. The Ten Commandments have always formed an objective basis for our legislation.

God Acts Throughout History

God is not merely a God who speaks, He is also a God who acts. He created the world—it did not just appear all by itself. He has constantly moved throughout history, and His intervention has always been supernatural.

For Moses, He parted the Red Sea so the Israelites could cross on dry land. For Joshua, the sun stood still over Gibeon and the moon over the Valley of Aijalon. The walls of Jericho fell supernaturally. Samson lifted the gates of a city on his shoulders, with supernatural strength. The three Hebrew men walked around in a fiery furnace without being hurt.

Daniel slept among lions whose mouths had been shut, and Elijah called down fire from heaven.

Jesus healed the sick, walked on the water, changed water into wine, and performed miracles with bread. Above all else, He was resurrected from the dead on the third day, having died on Calvary one day in history, for the sins of mankind. Peter healed a man at a gate in Jerusalem, Paul healed the sick on the island of Malta, and so on.

The Bible is full of supernatural, historical occurrences—points when a real God intervened and performed verifiable miracles. Believers have accepted this as fact throughout history. They have expected these things to continue happening on an ongoing basis, because God exists, speaks and acts.

Humanism has undermined and denied each of these three Biblical foundations, drawing the general public in a totally different direction.

Man—The Measure of Everything?

Humanism's starting point is not God, but man. According to humanistic thinking, man is not God's creation, he is just a highly developed animal. The world as a whole does not exist as a result of what God has done. Instead, the world has become what it is today, through spontaneous and random development.

According to humanistic thinking, there is no such thing as a fall into sin. Mankind is simply as it is, and therefore must be permitted to live out its every fantasy, inclination and desire, these being simply "human." As humans, we are not to be burdened with guilt. Man has not fallen from fellowship with God, but is in himself good.

According to humanistic thought, man is good. Therefore he should not be disciplined or punished, since this is judgmental and hinders his development. Setting limits is restrictive. Man must have the freedom to do what he himself deems to be right.

Because objective morality does not exist, no one behavior should be inhibited more than any other. Everything is relative, and therefore no one has the right to say that one form of behavior is better than the next. Humanism is built on the presupposition that God does not exist and that development is random. Therefore, it breeds a relative view of life.

Everything is relative. Nothing is fundamentally right or wrong, so it all depends what the individual himself thinks is correct. Subjective experience becomes extremely important. If it feels good, it is good. Man is the measure of everything. Actions are not wrong in and of themselves, only in relation to their consequences for the individual and society. And even this can vary, since "everything is relative."

The goal of mankind becomes self-realization, and with this reasoning whatever appears to prevent this from happening is labeled as "sin." This is why humanism is generally tolerant toward everything except the Christian faith. Faith in God is based on the premise that there is an absolute; that there are things that are objectively right and objectively wrong.

This causes humanism great distress, since it perceives everything as relative. The word "freedom," that we discussed earlier, is interpreted to mean "the absence of inhibitions and limitations." An absolute moral is rejected, and those morals that do exist are said to be derived only from the individual's personal experience, this of course being "different from one person to the next."

The punishment of criminals, for example, is no longer discussed. As a result, disorder and amorality become the normal behavior. This, if anything, is a sure way to lead society into chaos. The wild experiments of the sixties have resulted in a pattern known today as AIDS; a plague which society is helpless to control.

It is especially difficult to control when today's authorities have for decades supported the morality and behavior that has resulted in the present-day AIDS crisis. They hardly know which way to turn now, and can do nothing but offer a collection of pathetically vague, weak directives. They try closing their eyes, hoping that the monster will go away all by itself.

In spite of their premise that man is good, every humanist accepts the fact that the world in which we live is imperfect. However, the notion that this is because the individual has fallen into sin and now stands guilty before God is denied with fervor. The idea that man is in need of a personal Savior—Jesus Christ—is denied even more fiercely.

But because the problem remains, something must be done about it. Thus, mankind becomes his own savior, and the means to his salvation is knowledge. Through education, man is said to be elevated beyond prejudices and primitive behavior. Hence, vast sums of money have been spent in an attempt to save mankind through knowledge.

The Basis of Knowledge

Knowledge is important. Without it, man sinks into a superstitious, primitive existence. Wherever Christianity has come, man's knowledge has increased. True Christianity has always resisted superstition and ignorance, and emphasized the need for increased knowledge. It is interesting to note that in the wake of Christian culture the conditions were created which gave rise to scientific investigation and the advance of modern science.

However, like everything else, knowledge too must have a basis. Our minds give us the ability to collect facts, but at the same time we need help to interpret these facts. This help comes from God, the creator of everything and the One who has given us the ability to think. The Bible has never been opposed to thought; in fact, the opposite is true. First Corinthians 14:20 says, *In regard to evil be infants, but in your thinking be adults.*

According to the Bible, though, knowledge that is disconnected from its foundation in God becomes foolishness.

> For it is written: "I will destroy the wisdom of the wise; the intelligence of the intelligent I will frustrate." Where is the wise man? Where is the scholar? Where is the philosopher of this age? Has not God make foolish the wisdom of the world? For since in the wisdom of God the world through its wisdom did not know him, God was pleased through the foolishness of what was preached to save those who believe (1 Cor 1:19-21).

Psalm 14:1 boldly declares, *The fool says in his heart, "There is no God."* In other words, the Bible clearly proclaims that knowledge that denies the existence of God is nothing more than foolishness.

If the key that is needed to correctly interpret facts is missing, man will inevitable go wrong, in spite of how many facts he claims to have. Furthermore, if the premises of a system of thought are wrong, the conclusions will be wrong, no matter how many interesting concepts and facts the system may incorporate.

Knowledge alone does not change a person's morals or behavior. Highly educated individuals are still capable of criminal and immoral behavior and, in spite of their education, can become selfish and corrupt.

In this respect, current school policy in Sweden is now facing its greatest crisis. Even our authorities are aware of it. It is obvious that the system does not work. Breakdown and chaos drive many teachers to change careers. There is a catastrophic decrease in the level of education. Sweden came second to last in an international mathematics competition; the country of Swaziland came in last.

The experiments of the fifties and sixties, with their relative foundations, are facing inevitable failure. But any admittance of this failure would mean aiming at the underlying philosophy itself, and so these facts remain stubbornly denied.

A New Intolerance

Although humanism considers knowledge as its ideal, it is still extremely relative and experience oriented. This has had serious consequences on our school policy. The level of education has consistently decreased. Books have become smaller, pictures larger and texts more sparse.

The volume of knowledge has shrunk considerably, while at the same time society has become a more complicated place in which to live, thus requiring a greater amount of information. Humanism has become counterproductive toward its own ideals. Rather than emphasizing facts, it focuses on emotional experiences and general opinions.

A generation is growing up which pretends to have an opinion about everything. While demanding room to make these opinions known, behind the issues are very few real facts. Less care is taken to criticize sources and to remain unbiased and objective. As a result, emotional inclinations and subjective experiences gain weight.

This is the seedbed in which prejudices and preconceptions flourish, and where aggression is easily instigated. Here, too, a new intolerance is bred for anything that departs from the mass opinion.

Consequently, the journalism of evening papers and distorted monopolized television programs become the perfect media for disseminating lies and propaganda. The university axiom of the Middle Ages, which involved explaining an opponent's standpoint to the extent that one could recognize it and agree with it before attacking him, has long since been forgotten. Today, loaded phrases and emotionally charged expressions are given precedence over plain facts and objective analysis.

If the level of knowledge continues to decrease in Sweden, a climate of prejudice and a plebeian mentality will once again take over. An educational monopoly, with a completely secularized and relative foundation and an existential, emotional emphasis, has opened wide the doors for this kind of counter development.

Biblical faith has often been accused of being unscientific and intolerant. In fact, it is actually humanism that is so.

Humanism is built on a group of presumptions that are more or less unprovable. This makes it more like a religious system than an ideology that is based on facts. Its aim seems, at first glance, to be merely the denial of facts. The existence of mankind is explained without God, without the Fall and without the need for a Savior. In order to maintain credibility, the humanist is forced to be aggressively prejudiced against the fundamental Christian norms and dogmas.

Christianity is not causing chaos in values, the breakdown of morals and endless human tragedy—it is secular humanism. Christianity does not discard man's value and make him a meaningless being— humanism does. Christianity does not do away with the preservation of human life, but from abortion to euthanasia, humanism based on atheism does.

In spite of its magnificent slogans and idealistic programs, secular humanism is facing a reality that cannot be explained away. Its ideas are suffering shipwreck against the great cliffs of reality. This is humanism's dilemma. Despite all that it claims, as Psalm 111:10 says, *The fear of the Lord is the beginning of wisdom.*

6

Words,
Their Meaning and Use

Words are important. They are containers of power.
The Bible tells us that *death and life are in the*
power of the tongue (Prov 18:21 NKJV). When God
created the world, He did so with words. He spoke,
and it came into being; He commanded and it stood
firm (see Ps 33:9).

Words carry either life or death. They have the
power to create, set free and heal, or to tear down
and destroy. The words of God are filled with life.
Jesus said, *The words I have spoken to you are spirit*
and they are life (John 6:63).

Psalm 107:20 says: *He sent forth his word and*
healed them; he rescued them from the grave. God's
words, which come as a revelation from His throne,
are true and valid. They carry within themselves
the ability to accomplish all that they promise. God's
promises are true and His Spirit confirms His Word
so that it accomplishes what it was sent to do (see
Isa 55:11).

Words Relay More Than Just Facts

We see then that words carry life or death, truth
or lies, depending on their source. The Gospel of
Jesus Christ must therefore be proclaimed with
boldness, because He is the way, the truth and the
life (see John 14:6). The Word of God destroys lies

and sets people free, in spite of how uncomfortable it may feel when it comes.

We are perpetually surrounded with words. Without them we would be unable to communicate with the world around us. Words convey knowledge and information that enable us to live. However, words convey more than just this. Apart from merely containing facts, they are also emotive, they are full of feeling and convey an atmosphere.

Words touch our frames of reference and our individual experiences. A word with positive implications for one person may have negative implications for another. Words may lose their original meaning or factual content, becoming emotionally charged and taking on new, suggestive implications.

Propaganda and misinformation (misleading information) have abused words in this manner. The general public defines the words they hear based not on facts but on emotions. Words have always been used in this suggestive manner within politics, the mass media and advertising.

The aim is to quickly influence people to move in one particular direction. In this context, words are used to trap and mislead rather than to inform.

Words are influential and this is not necessarily negative. Jesus was highly influential when He preached. People committed their lives to the Kingdom of God. The contents of His words, however, were true. His words were spirit and life, and what He said was based on reality.

His enemy, however, used lies as weapons. Although the witnesses at Jesus' trial were unable to get their testimonies to agree, and though they contradicted one another (see Matt 26:59-62) by speaking emotionally charged words, they were still able to whip up the atmosphere to the extent that Jesus was finally crucified (see Matt 27:18,20-23). The crowd was further incited through the persuasion of the high priests and they began shouting, "Crucify him, Crucify him."

Words are therefore extremely meaningful, and the influence they exert on people is colossal.

"Mudslinging" is commonplace in political and religious debates. Something completely different is meant with the words that are used, and rather than bothering to define them, they are used entirely for their emotive value. This method of appealing to people's emotions is primitive and dangerous. Modern propaganda is based on the same general principle as was developed by Goebbels in Nazi Germany.

Goebbels claimed that if a lie were repeated enough times—if it was said that a Jew was a detestable swine, for instance—this would eventually become an established truth in people's consciousness. A stronghold was built which made people almost completely unreceptive to the truth. Truth became what they believed it to be, like the man who said, "I've already made up my mind, don't confuse me with the facts."

Another way of manipulating people with words is by mixing them with an ingredient of truth. The element of truth is recognizable and acts as a water-slide so that people are carried away and accept the rest without reservation.

The Battle for the Truth

There is a battle underway today for the souls of men and women, and words—whether they be true or false—are the primary means whereby people are influenced.

An antagonist may, therefore, use words in a very unworthy manner. Rather than clearly defining both his own viewpoint and that of his opponent, to the satisfaction of everyone involved, generalizations and emotive terms are used. Such words horrify the uninitiated and cause the defendant to blink with surprise, unable even to recognize the viewpoints under siege as his own.

It is one thing when this happens among the man-on-the-street, or as a part of gossip over a cup of coffee, but it is quite another thing when it involves national media.

The honesty that sticks to the facts and refrains from manipulation is, unfortunately, quite unusual. Evening papers revel in dishonest behavior; but one can hardly expect anything else from them. Sometimes their hunger for profit and sensationalism seems to know no bounds. What is worse, though, is seeing serious politicians and investigative television, radio and university staff lower themselves to employ such methods.

These people are responsible for their words. What they say weighs much more than the words of the common man and, therefore, a higher standard of ethics is expected from them. Words like "right wing," "reactionary" and "fascist" are misused in this way. Usually the left wing uses these terms completely indiscriminately to mean anything that appears to stand to their right, or to refer to those with differing opinions, in spite of what the opinion in question may be.

I remember when I studied theology at the University of Uppsala, Sweden. It was surprising to see how carelessly the word "fundamentalist" was used by certain professors. In principle, anyone who disagreed with the lecturer was called one. It was hardly used as an expression of fact, but rather as an insult.

You were a threat if you were at all suspected of being one, and students would go to great lengths to avoid being accused of something so stupid, foolish and narrow-minded. For the students, the original meaning of the word "fundamentalist" had become equivalent with "a complete idiot who is absolutely unacceptable as a prospective priest." And no one wanted to be that!

Lies as Weapons

The mass media has begun to use such words in this manner during the past few years. One evening paper, for example, called the South African pastor Ray McCauley a "fascist priest," in spite of the fact that he had publicly dissociated himself from apartheid. This, of course, remained unmentioned. Truth and honesty had long been forgotten in this case.

We could easily list the accusations that have found their way into the mass media during the past few years, one more serious and bizarre than the next, but that is not the aim of this book. The purpose is to point out the serious lack of respect for the truth that seems to rule in our country. The eighth commandment says, *You shall not give false testimony against your neighbor* (Ex 20:16).

When politicians and others in positions of responsibility resort to using lies in their attempt to gain political influence, a country is in danger. Hosea 4:1 declares, *the Lord has a charge to bring against you who live in the land: There is **no faithfulness**, no love, no acknowledment of God in the land.*

*A false witness will not go unpunished, and he who **pours out lies** will not go free* (Prov 19:5).

It is vital that both the standard of political debate and the individual's respect for the truth is raised. If lies are promoted as a political means and words are carefully manipulated so that the listener fails to receive a true meaning, then a whole nation can be led astray. The outcome is particularly serious.

Communist ideology has always retained the right to use words in this way. According to the communists, objective truth is non-existent and ideas are historical facts that can be altered to suit their needs. This is done in order to reach their ultimate goal—eventual world domination by socialism, a goal that has by no means been forgotten.

This flagrant violation of the truth has always been a part of dictatorships. It is extremely serious when the same methods become common in a democratic society, where freedom of opinion and freedom of expression are the cornerstones of its continued existence. A country brings disgrace on itself when it forsakes the truth.

Words are valuable and the right to have and express opinions is precious. We should never take this for granted. It is a democratic privilege that should not be defiled and dishonored by being used in the service of spreading lies and promoting prejudice.

Jesus talks about the importance of words in Matthew 12:36-37 when He says, *But I tell you that men will have to give account on the day of judgment for **every** careless word they have spoken. For by your words you will be acquitted, and by your words you will be condemned.*

The future of every country lies in a return to the truth, a respect for the proper use of words and a bold proclamation of words that are filled with spirit and life. As a result, the whole nation will enjoy life.

7

The Question of Defense

We mentioned in Chapter 2 that the task of a government is to uphold internal and external defense. Few people find the concept of internal defense problematic. Almost everyone would agree that a police presence is necessary to uphold order within a country.

Whether they are believers or unbelievers, every politician in Sweden today also agrees on the necessity of having an external national defense. There is widespread unity on the question of defense. Almost everyone agrees on the need for a national defense that satisfactorily carries out its task of defending our country against trespassers.

Both the government and its opposition agree on this fundamental question. On the other hand, however, the outlook among Christians is divided, many being highly skeptical toward national defense. The real question is whether or not such a view is actually Biblical.

It is obvious that a Christian, and almost everyone else for that matter, does not want to kill or advocate violence. Violence is terrible and has a demoralizing effect on society. A society full of video violence breeds a generation that believes physical violence is a legitimate means of solving conflicts.

In Exodus 20:13 the Bible says, *You shall not murder.* No one has the right to take another person's life—and those who do so should be punished.

Neither do private individuals have any right to take the law into their own hands in an attempt to do justice. Citizens have left this up to the state.

In Romans 13:4 Paul says of the authorities that *he does not bear the sword for nothing. He is God's servant, an agent of wrath to bring punishment on the wrongdoer.*

The authorities have been given a means of external force, one that actually includes violence, in order to preserve order within society. When the situation arises, the police must use violence to stop criminals from causing people harm.

However, in Paul's day no distinction was made between internal and external defense, as is the case today. Soldiers carried out both of these tasks. Their job was to defend against both inner and outer enemies for the continued existence of the country. We see, then, that Romans 13:4 applies as much to external defense as it does to police power.

We should also notice in this scripture that Paul does not tell us to refuse to be involved in defense. An objection commonly raised to military service is that many of the early Christians refused to join the Roman army. Their refusal, however, was not for political reasons, but because Roman soldiers were obliged to worship and swear allegiance to Caesar. This was impossible for those who had Jesus as their Lord. They simply refused to worship anyone other than Jesus.

Luke 3:14 relates the story of the soldiers who came to John the Baptist to repent and confess their sins. When they asked him what to do, he did not tell them to put away their weapons and become pacifists. Instead, he said, *don't extort money and*

don't accuse people falsely—be content with your pay.
In other words, carry out your duties in an exemplary manner and be honest and careful. There was no mention that they should give up their profession.

Christian Pacifism?

The influence of pacifism has been widespread among Christians in Sweden, as has the influence of socialism. Swedish socialism differs from its relatives in other countries on this point in particular. The military emphasis in most other countries is greater.

Examples of such countries include Angola, Mozambique, Cuba, Vietnam, Ethiopia and other states that are actively supported by Sweden. In addition, a number of these countries are dictatorial regimes and not true democracies.

Pacifism is by no means a Christian doctrine. Its premise is that man is fundamentally good—that if only man would begin to put down his weapons, others would follow suit. This is an idealistic view that is certainly nice, but it is both unrealistic and unscriptural.

The scriptural world view is that we live in a fallen world and that apart from God man is a sinner and not at all good. The love of God and the forgiving grace of the Gospel are necessary to bring him to salvation. The government has been given forcible means to preserve society and its law and order, to prevent greater evil.

The day is coming when the sword will be beaten into a ploughshare (see Isa 2:4), but not before the Prince of Peace, Jesus Christ, returns. There will be no lasting peace on this earth without Him—and

He is coming! However, when Jesus talked about His return and the end of the age, He clearly said that we would hear of wars and rumors of wars, and that *nation will rise against nation, and kingdom against kingdom* (Matt 24:6-7).

In the Book of Revelation, Jesus' return is clearly portrayed as a day when He defeats Antichrist's great military forces on the battlefield of Armageddon (see Rev 16:14-15; 19:17-21). In no way does the Bible make room for the pacifism so common among Christians. The basis of such a view is not Biblical.

If, for reasons of conscience, a Christian chooses not to take part in military service, our state law makes provision for this and he is allowed to act according to his convictions. But from a Biblical point of view, this hardly gives him the right to question those Christians who choose to participate in military service. He is even less entitled to criticize or disparage the defense that is an integral part of his government's commission to uphold the well-being and security of his country.

Effective Defense is Necessary

The Swedish national defense system is in a state of crisis. Subsidies have decreased drastically in relation to the increase in spending. Since the beginning of the 1970s, Sweden has reduced its armament by practically 50%. Both the Marines and the Air Force have been halved, and the same is virtually true for the Army. In addition, much of the equipment is ageing. Most of the artillery and many of the jeeps were manufactured in the 1950s.

Several prominent military officers have clearly stated that the national defense is unable to satisfactorily carry out its duties; in the case of external attack, it would be completely inadequate to protect the Swedish populace. This is extremely alarming. If we are to have a defense, it should at least be one that is adequate.

The clumsy submarine searches in recent years, with their constant standstills, make our incompetence, or even unwillingness to defend ourselves, only too clear to the rest of the world and to our potential adversaries.

Spies who defect, and top-secret documents that are available for anyone to look at, demonstrate an extreme laxity and compromise that is almost enough to incite suspicion. The same can be said for the authorities' refusal to mention the Soviet Union by name, in regard to the violation of our territory by its submarines.

For several years, a peace movement has been spreading throughout a number of western countries. Despite the fact that its ideas occasionally border on the official policies of the Soviet Union, many Christians have become involved in this movement. Disarmament is short-sightedly thought to be beneficial, especially in relation to Swedish defense.

What is ignored, however, is the fact that we have a neighbor in the East who has not changed his objectives, merely his tactics when it has been appropriate. Though called the "Sea of Peace," the Baltic Sea is filled with nuclear arms and submarines.

The notion that because we are insignificant, politically neutral and harmless ("no one would want ever to hurt us"), is nothing short of wishful thinking. Clear proof of this lies in the less than casual interest our "neighbor in the East" demonstrates toward our country.

This interest does not come only in the form of official visits or unlawful submarine visits. It includes everything from diplomatic personnel actively involved in spying, Polish merchants selling oil paintings and strategically seeking out Swedish fighter pilots in their homes, to Russian trucks that circle around military bases and keep to the outskirts of large maneuvers, planes that "navigate wrongly," divers who appear in the archipelago, and so on.

These things have been kept quiet and more or less explained away. Our Secretary of Defense has personally stated that no steps will be taken to control the presence of Russian reconnaissance vehicles in Sweden. This is perhaps not so remarkable, when it seems that we fail to understand where the Russian submarines come from, despite the fact that their minisubmarines are cutting underwater cables that belong to our Coast Guard.

Sweden is Strategic

Why such a sudden interest in Sweden? Because the information necessary to carry out a possible invasion is being systematically compiled. Spying is not done just for fun. It is a highly conscious gathering of facts related to our defense, which is coupled with public charm—offensives of peace and glasnost.

Sweden is strategically located—and we must be aware of our position, not only spiritually, but physically and geographically as well. In both Sweden and the rest of Scandinavia, military expertise concurs that a careful and deliberate collection of military information by the Eastern state, is underway in Sweden.

There is also agreement that this is the first step in the planning of a potential invasion. Such an invasion would be necessary to secure Soviet political and military interests in any possible future crisis with NATO.

Just as we must pray for our country and protect its borders spiritually, we need to also protect ourselves in the natural. Our strong reluctance to have an effective defense is our enemy's greatest advantage over us.

A Christian who does not want national defense might as well do away with the police force. If he is opposed to a defense, perhaps he should also remove the locks from his house and car and put his money on the street outside his home. Surely no one is quite that naive. But we are often incredibly naive when it comes to both the spiritual and natural security of our country.

If we are to have a national defense, it should at least be adequate. Therefore, I believe God will send a revival among soldiers and officers, so they will be born again, become more effective and be led by the Lord in their task of defending Sweden.

This revival will not make them more bloodthirsty and murderous, as many have misinterpreted it to mean. Instead, they will be better able to carry out their responsibilities, just as politicians, administrative personnel, police and others, function better when they have peace with God and access to His Spirit. Then they will be able to pray and expose security leaks and traitors within our defense system.

Defense or Disgrace

Freedom is something precious. We have enjoyed this privilege for so long that we have become spoiled and almost arrogant. Freedom is not taken for granted in most other countries in the world. Many countries, like those of the eastern bloc, for example, have hade no freedom whatsoever.

Freedom of choice, freedom of opinion, and other fundamental democratic rights are extremely valuable. However, there is no guarantee that we will always be able to enjoy them. Sweden has been blessed by being able to avoid war for more than one hundred and fifty years, something that is quite unusual, internationally speaking.

As a result, we have almost fallen asleep and taken on the "it-will-never-happen-to-us" mentality. However, the world is not lying at Sweden's feet, looking up to us in adoration with the notion that we are completely innocent and wonderful. The "Swedish model" is not so fantastic that it cannot be infringed on. We saw violence force its way closer to our everyday lives through the tragic death of our former prime minister, Olof Palme.

Having not experienced international conflict for so many years, we are at risk of becoming unsuspecting and naive. And if a conflict were to arise, there is a further risk that, rather than defending ourselves, we would be more inclined to submit and sell our freedom, to preserve some measure of security.

Even our police force has had an official change of regulations. In the past, they were ordered to resist an invader. Now, however, the policy is to assist an invading force in the reduction of bloodshed.

In First Samuel 11:1-2, the Bible talks about Nahash the Ammonite who besieged the city of Jabesh, a town that belonged to the Israelites. The men of Jabesh said to Nahash, *"Make a treaty with us, and we will be subject to you."* But Nahash the Ammonite replied, *"I will make a treaty with you only on the condition that I gouge out the right eye of every one of you and so bring disgrace on all of Israel."*

There is a principle here that applies both spiritually and physically. When threatened, the people of Jabesh were ready to sell their freedom and independence in return for security and the form of a peace treaty. They were able to do this if they wished, but apart from the loss of freedom itself, the price was the loss of everyone's right eye.

The attitude that gives up, to gain peace and security, means the loss of something precious for every person, as well as a state of disgrace coming over the land.

First Samuel 11:6 tells us the conclusion of the distressing situation faced by the people of Jabesh. The Spirit of God, the Bible declares, came powerfully upon Saul, so that he burned with anger, mustered the people and scattered the Ammonites.

Freedom is Worth Defending

We have a natural desire to defend ourselves, to resist attacks and to protect freedom as something valuable. This can be applied both spiritually and physically. The freedom we enjoy here in Sweden is extremely precious. One of its many consequences is the freedom to spread the Gospel throughout the entire world. If this freedom were lost, the results would be serious, not only for Sweden itself, but for the rest of the world.

An effective defense and a strong motivation for defense is the best thing a country can possess. In spite of this, a Christian who is in support of a strong defense is often considered bloodthirsty and militant in western circles. But this is absurd. If this were true, our parliament and government would also be bloodthirsty.

No true Christian promotes violence or desires to see war. The point is, we must have a clear, Biblical view of both man himself and the world we live in, so we can support the role of the government in this area.

Sweden is a wonderful country. It is a privilege to be able to live here and enjoy the freedom it offers. It is a blessing to have a democratic system that respects the fundamental rights of humanity. This is something well worth defending.

Any depreciation or undermining of our defense, any demoralizing influence, will only hinder us should the integrity and independence of our country come under threat. We are either incredibly naive, or consciously corrupt, to fail to notice the clear signals that tell us that this is presently the case.

8

At Election Time—What Should One Do?

As individual believers and as a church, we hold the responsibility for the government of our country. The way we conduct ourselves has a direct effect on the spiritual climate of the nation. In this regard, there are three practical areas we are to be involved in concerning our country and its future.

First, we should pray.

> I urge then, first of all, that requests, prayers, intercession and thanksgiving be made for everyone—for kings and all those in authority, that we may live peaceful and quiet lives in all godliness and holiness. This is good and pleases God our Savior, who wants all men to be saved and to come to a knowledge of the truth (1 Tim 2:1-4).

Here Paul says that we should *first of all* (meaning above all else, or as top priority) pray for our rulers. We are not to constantly complain, grumble or criticize, but to pray instead. Because we have often failed to do this, we have received the government we deserve.

Why should we pray for them? So that they can come under the influence of the Holy Spirit and be able to make correct decisions. So they can know the fear of the Lord and therefore be afraid to legislate ungodly laws that will destroy our country. God is free to influence them when we pray, for *the*

*king's heart is in the hand of the Lord; he directs
it like a watercourse wherever he pleases* (Prov 21:1).

We have seen this exemplified at Word of Life
Christian School, our private elementary and
secondary school. Authorities on every level were
against us, right up to the government itself. They
did not want to grant us permission for the school,
until they were finally forced to do so in order to
avoid reprimand in the European Court.

Prayer worked a miracle, even when under great
opposition, and we were able to bless the government
and our Cultural Minister for his proper ruling.

We pray and thank God for our government every
week in our Sunday morning meetings here at Word
of Life Church. We speak about them in accordance
with the Word of God. We do not merely complain
and grumble, we bless them and lift them up instead,
knowing that their work is of great importance, that
it is difficult, and that they are subject to a great
deal of pressure.

When we pray for them, according to First
Timothy 2:2, the result is that we *may live peaceful
and quiet lives in all godliness and holiness.* This
is not so we can be left alone to drink our cup of
coffee in peace and quiet. No, it means that we can
live so that we are able to carry out whatever we
have been called to do, without hindrance. As
Christians, we are called to preach the Gospel. Verse
4 tells us that God "wants all men to be saved and
to come to a knowledge of the truth."

Our purpose, then, is to pray for our rulers, so
that their method of government maximizes an
opening for the Gospel, and so that as believers we
are not disturbed, hindered or persecuted by the

authorities. Our prayers are extremely effective. We need to be aware of this.

If a government is completely unreceptive to the Gospel, or persists in passing laws which lead the country away from God, we can pray for God to remove them and to give us a government that is positively disposed toward the Gospel instead.

Daniel 2:19-22 says:

> Then Daniel praised the God of heaven and said: "Praise be to the name of God for ever and ever; wisdom and power are his. He changes times and seasons; he sets up kings and deposes them. He gives wisdom to the wise and knowledge to the discerning. He reveals deep and hidden things; he knows what lies in darkness, and light dwells with him."

Second, we should act and confront.

This is especially true when the government attempts to violate our rights or lead us in a wrong direction. Paul was highly conscious of his two distinct citizenships. His first citizenship was in the Kingdom of God (see Phil 3:20), and his second was in the Roman Empire.

Being a citizen of Rome carried with it certain responsibilities, as well as a number of privileges. Paul often took advantage of these rights. He was not so "superspiritual" that he "just prayed," he also took action.

Once, the Jews tried to kill him, and Roman soldiers who had believed the Jews' accusations were ready to scourge him. Paul asked the soldiers, *Is it legal for you to flog a Roman citizen who hasn't even been found guilty?* (Acts 22:25). He was aware of his rights and did not allow the soldiers simply to take advantage of him.

You also need to know your rights as a citizen, so the authorities do not run you over, whether on purpose or by accident. At Word of Life, we have seen the importance of understanding the law, to carefully protect our rights, especially in the case of our Christian school. Had we not taken action, the authorities would have acted unjustly, in one instance by wrongly attempting to withhold support from the school.

When Paul was jailed in Philippi without cause, and the rulers discovered their mistake and attempted to tone down the situation, Paul he was not mild, servile or compliant. Instead he said, *They beat us publicly without a trial, even though we are Roman citizens, and threw us into prison. And now do they want to get rid of us quietly? No! Let them come themselves and escort us out* (Acts 16:37).

Paul would not give them an inch. On another occasion, when the Jews demanded that he be handed over for trial in Jerusalem, Paul refused and used his right to appeal to Caesar (see Acts 25:11-12). On a number of other occasions, Paul stood before the high court, the Sanhedrin, before Felix and king Agrippa. In each of these confrontations he defended himself.

He did not just pray. He explained, confronted and used his rights as a citizen when wrongly accused, mistreated or pushed to the side.

Third, we must take advantage of our right to vote.

Sweden is a democracy, something that is extremely precious. Democracy is government by the people. The people elect representatives to rule on major issues and thus the government is formed.

We grant the government a certain, limited amount of power to do what we, as individuals, are unable to do ourselves. Their task is to legislate into existence and uphold the freedom and privileges that God has intended for every human being.

Democracy is without question the best form of government, but, as with every system, it has its limitations. Democracy also places a greater demand on the individual citizen. He or she must become involved in the creation and formation of plans of action, as well as in the decision making process itself.

If the citizens fail to do this, many decisions will be made without their knowledge or involvement. Therefore, it is vital that the local church stays in touch with appointed officials and regularly takes account of their response to various issues.

Find out what your representatives really think. Communicate with them and compel them to answer for their actions. Demand to know the motivation behind their vote on various issues. If they vote against something that directly affects your church's position in the community, investigate the votes of other members within the same party. If they have voted against the party consensus, and to your disadvantage, take it up with their superiors.

As Christians, we have thousands of votes that carry great significance at election time. We must not neglect this, but rather let our influence be made known in whatever way we can.

Should we vote? Yes, certainly. This is one of the duties of citizenship. It is irresponsible not to vote, just as it is irresponsible not to pray for our country.

Those who want to preserve democracy must follow its rules.

How should we vote? We must first realize that no political party is perfect. Each party has its weaknesses. They all contain members who are unbelievers, perhaps even those who are against revival Christianity altogether.

When voting, it is important to look at more than just the individual issues. Every party represents certain platforms or positions that are positive. However, the real question is much deeper. It concerns the underlying ideology that directs the party and the potential development of such a philosophy.

"But my vote won't do any good," you may say. Of course it will! It's remarkable to see just how few votes can determine who wins in local and national elections. Your vote is by no means insignificant.

Which party should I vote for? You must decide this for yourself. For this reason you ought to take time to pray before you vote. Remember, God is able to use a government even when its members are not personal believers. The real issue is whether their general direction is in line with Biblical principles, or whether their purposes are in clear opposition to these standards.

Find out, therefore, where the party in question stands on various issues, especially those that affect the furtherance of the Gospel. However, do not let the issues themselves decide for you. It is wrong to vote for a party that will have a decidedly negative effect on our society, one that will lead us in an anti-Christian direction.

We need a government that will be a blessing for our country in every way and on every level—and it is within your power to see that this comes to pass.

Appendix I

A Word to Politicians

Your position is very important. You hold offices that have been ordained by God, and because of your position you are to be respected and honored. Believers everywhere are praying for you, blessing you and wishing you well.

Your position is one of incredible responsibility. You hold the country in your hands. Its future is determined by how well you carry out the tasks to which you have been appointed. Negligence on your part carries with it far-reaching, negative consequences for the entire nation.

Through a democratic election, the people of this country have appointed you as their representatives. In your position as their ministers, you are a part of an institution that God has initiated. You stand accountable for your decisions; before the people in this present age, and before God in eternity.

In the Gospel of John 15:5 (NKJV), Jesus says, *without Me you can do nothing.* This scripture applies to all of us, yourselves included. You will never be able to fully carry out your commission without the help of Jesus Christ. He has the wisdom you need to rightly lead this country. If you ask Him for it He will freely give it to you. Include Him in your counsel, and a fresh purity, strength and wisdom will fill you, and the decisions you make will result in previously unimagined success.

This country is in a state of crisis, and you are more aware of this than any one else. Therefore, be fearless in your task. Do not silence your conscience but let it lead you. Do not hide the truth but receive it, even if it should come from outside of your own party. Humble yourself beneath the mighty hand of God and He will lift you up and speak to you.

Our nation is a democracy and we thank God for this fact. Preserve democracy and utilize its capabilities and advantages to the good of the country.

Always remember that believers throughout the nation are praying for you, and God always hears our prayers. God bless you!

Appendix II

God Bless Our Country!

Father, in the Name of Jesus, we lift our country before you. We thank you for the country you have given us. You have said in your Word, in Second Chronicles 7:14 that *if my people, who are called by my name, will humble themselves and pray and seek my face and turn from their wicked ways, then I will hear from heaven and will forgive their sin and will heal their land.*

As Christians, and as the Body of Christ, we have not prayed for our country, or watched over it as we should have. We confess this as sin and we turn from our selfish ways. We come to you to pray for and guard this country in the spirit.

We lift up and bless our government. We thank you for it, for our Parliament and for every political representative who stands for the people. We lift them up before you and ask that their decisions correspond with your decisions.

We pray that a fear of the Lord will come over them that causes them to respect your laws and commands, so that they dare not raise themselves up against what you have thought or planned. We pray protection for their minds so that the truth, and not lies, may direct their paths.

In the Name of Jesus, we pray for the work of the Holy Spirit in our government and across this land, bringing repentance, revival, blessing and success. May this country be all that God has designed it to be.

We proclaim freedom for this country and freedom for what God has planned and intended. We pray for God's angels to protect our borders and guard what God wants to do here.

We call on the cleansing blood of Jesus for forgiveness, purification, protection and liberty throughout the land.

We praise you, Lord, that you hear our prayers and when we pray for the government, you bless our country so the Gospel may be freely preached and received by the people, resulting in salvation and deliverance for the whole nation.

We thank you that your Spirit will be poured out over this country. We thank you that signs and wonders will be widespread, and that people will understand that you are indeed a good God. Thank you that Jesus is alive today, willing and able to change people's lives.

We confess Jesus as Lord over this country.

We bless this country in the Name of Jesus.

Amen.

Other Books by Ulf Ekman

A Life of Victory
The guidance, help and inspiration you need to put God's Word first. Fifty-four chapters, each dealing with a particular area of the believer's life. 288 pages

The Authority in the Name of Jesus
When you receive a revelation of what the name of Jesus really means, you will have boldness like never before.
Booklet, 32 pages

Destroy the Works of the Devil
Jesus came to earth to destroy the works of the devil. His death on the cross struck Satan a death blow. Jesus triumphed over him and won the victory for YOU!
Booklet, 32 pages

Faith that Overcomes the World
Explains how faith arises, how it becomes operational, and what makes it grow. 144 pages

Financial Freedom
A thorough, biblical study on money, riches and material possessions. 128 pages

God Wants to Heal Everyone
Discover the wonderful fact that God's will is to heal everyone—including you.
Booklet, 32 pages

The Power in the New Creation
A new dimension of victorious living awaits you. The Lord is with you, Mighty Warrior! Booklet, 32 pages

The Jews—People of the Future
Clarifies basic truths about the people and the land. Historical facts and Biblical prophecies combine to reveal the fulfillment of God's End-time Plan. 160 pages

The Prophetic Ministry
"Provides essential guideposts for the operation of the prophetic ministry today." From the Foreword by Demos Shakarian. 224 pages

Available from your local Christian bookstore, or order direct from the publisher:

Word of Life Publications
Box 17, S-751 03 Uppsala, Sweden
Box 46108, Minneapolis, MN 55446, USA
Box 641, Marine Parade, Singapore 9144